Who am I?

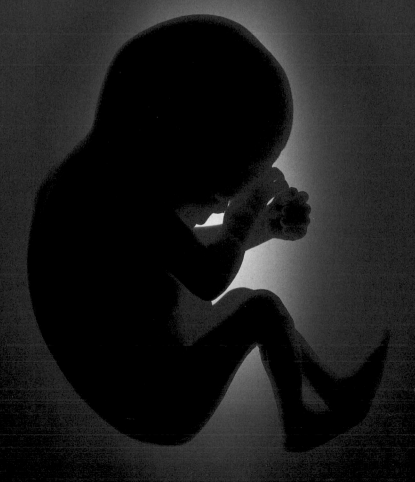

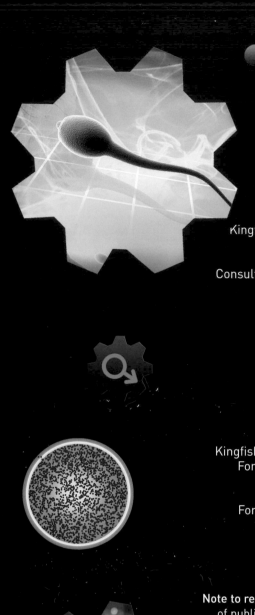

KINGFISHER
LONDON & NEW YORK

Copyright © Kingfisher 2012
Published in the United States by Kingfisher,
175 Fifth Ave., New York, NY 10010
Kingfisher is an imprint of Macmillan Children's Books, London.
All rights reserved.

Consultant: Holly Cave, curator, *Who Am I?* gallery, Science Museum,
London, UK
Illustrations by: Peter Bull Art Studio

Distributed in the U.S. and Canada by Macmillan,
175 Fifth Ave., New York, NY 10010

Library of Congress Cataloging-in-Publication data
has been applied for.

ISBN: 978-0-7534-6711-4

Kingfisher books are available for special promotions and premiums.
For details contact: Special Markets Department, Macmillan,
175 Fifth Ave., New York, NY 10010.

For more information, please visit www.kingfisherbooks.com

Printed in China
1 3 5 7 9 8 6 4 2
1TR/0112/WKT/UG/140MA

Note to readers: The website addresses listed in this book are correct at time
of publishing. However, due to the ever-changing nature of the Internet,
website addresses and content can change. Websites can contain links that
are unsuitable for children. The publisher cannot be held responsible for
changes in website addresses or content or for information obtained through
third-party websites. We strongly advise that Internet searches should be
supervised by an adult.

Who am I?

Richard Walker

KINGFISHER
NEW YORK

Contents

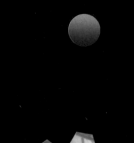

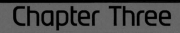

a ring-tailed lemur,
Madagascar

Being human

What does it mean to be human?
The simple answer is that we belong
to the human species, Homo sapiens. Ours
is one of more than one million named
species, or types, of animals on Earth. But
there's more to being human than that.

Compared with most animal species,
humans are recent arrivals—we evolved,
or appeared, only 200,000 years ago.
We stand apart from other animals
because of the size of our brain.

Our relatively big brain has
given us the intelligence
to adapt to and exploit
different environments.
We are able to communicate
and be sociable, creative, and
cultural. We are successful . . .
we are human!

We are animals

This lemur is a primate,
as are chimps and humans.
Primates are mammals—furry
animals that feed their young
milk—that have forward-facing eyes
and gripping fingers. But although
we share these features with our
primate relatives, there's a world
of difference between them and us.

We are social

People live and cooperate in
groups based on their immediate
families and other relationships—for
example, schools, workplaces, clubs, and
neighborhoods. We each have our own place
within such groups, or societies. In any social
group, those of us with more experience offer
protection, support, and guidance to those of
us who are younger or less knowledgeable.

**Women in
Zanzibar work
together to
catch fish.**

We communicate

The many different ways we use to communicate make us unique. As well as the body language and facial expressions that reveal our emotions, we use spoken and written language. With words, we can spread ideas and pass on knowledge to the next generation.

Signs inform pedestrians and traffic at a busy intersection in Tokyo, Japan.

We have culture

Whether we are rainforest-dwelling hunter-gatherers or big-city bankers, we all have our own culture, determined by how we behave, what we believe, and how we understand the world. There are many cultures in the world, but all share common features. Religion, or a belief in a higher, supernatural being, is one way that many of us make sense of life.

We are creative

Engineering, technology, science, art and design . . . humans possess an amazing range of unique and creative skills. All are the result of our extraordinary intelligence and our ability to think, imagine, and solve problems.

A father and daughter enjoy the Hindu festival of Holi.

Technological know-how has taken humans into space.

Inuit people dress to survive Arctic conditions.

We adapt

One reason our species has been so successful is that we have adapted to many different habitats, from the heat of the Sahara Desert to the freezing wastes of the Arctic. We've done this thanks to all sorts of inventions, talents, and technologies, including clothes, housing, heating, and agriculture.

Yoga is one way we explore our sense of self.

Being me

What does it mean to be me? Or you? What gives you your own identity and makes you that little bit different from the other seven billion humans on Earth?

You may have things in common with other people, but there's no one else exactly like you. Your specific thoughts, memories, perceptions, motives, friendships, likes and dislikes, skills, failings, and problems are all special to you.

You were shaped and molded by the DNA instructions in your cells and by your upbringing and surroundings. That exact combination is unique . . . just like you!

I am self-aware
Each of us has our own consciousness, that feeling of self-awareness that all humans experience. Being self-aware means that you can recognize yourself as an individual. It gives you an idea of yourself that includes what you think of your abilities and how you think others view you. Self-awareness also helps you appreciate your past, present, and future.

Artistic creativity is an aspect of our intelligence.

I am intelligent
We tend to think of someone being intelligent if they're very smart. But all of us are intelligent because we all think, learn, and experience the world around us. Intelligence isn't only one thing. It is a combination of skills that includes artistic, mathematical, musical, and language abilities. Each of us has our own individual set of skills.

I have a personality

Are you noisy and outgoing or quiet and withdrawn? Do you like new experiences or are you wary of them? Do you get angry easily or are you generally calm? These are just some of the features that together determine your personality. The uniqueness of your personality is recognized by your family and friends, and it underpins how you react to life experiences.

Skateboarding—popular with people who have adventurous personalities!

I have my own identity

Your identity is defined by how you see yourself, how you express yourself to others, and how others see you. It is shaped by all sorts of features—including the way you dress—that together make you unique. Your identity depends on the genes you inherit from your parents, your life experiences, and the culture you live in.

Clothes can express our identity.

A carving of Dzunukwa, a witch who features in stories told by native peoples from northwestern Canada.

I have an imagination

Your imagination is part of the private, inner world that you can escape into. In your imagination, you can think about, see, and experience new ideas. You use your imagination when you make up a story and also when you listen to stories and myths that other people have made up. In your imagination, you may meet all sorts of scary situations and monsters!

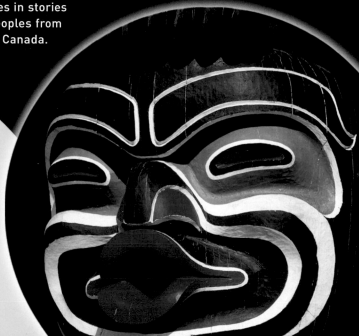

Am I . . . ?

Find out more about who you are by completing the personality quiz that runs through the book. It starts on this page and continues on pages 30, 50, 70, and 90.

Extrovert or introvert?
Whether you love excitement and fun (extrovert) or are more wary and less outgoing (introvert) is one aspect of your personality.

1. My dream vacation would involve:
a) snowboarding and bungee jumping
b) sunbathing on the beach and going snorkeling
c) visiting a museum with a friend

2. I enjoy spending my time with:
a) a large group of people, some of them friends
b) a small group of people I know
c) one or two really close friends

3. I would much prefer to:
a) do something dangerous, even if it gets me into trouble
b) try something risky, but only if I know I'm going to be safe
c) avoid taking chances and stick with something secure

4. When it comes to staying in touch, I like:
a) making long phone calls to friends
b) sending text messages every day to friends
c) sending occasional e-mails to close friends

Go to page 90 to find out if you're an extrovert or an introvert or go to page 30 to find out if you're conscientious or disorganized.

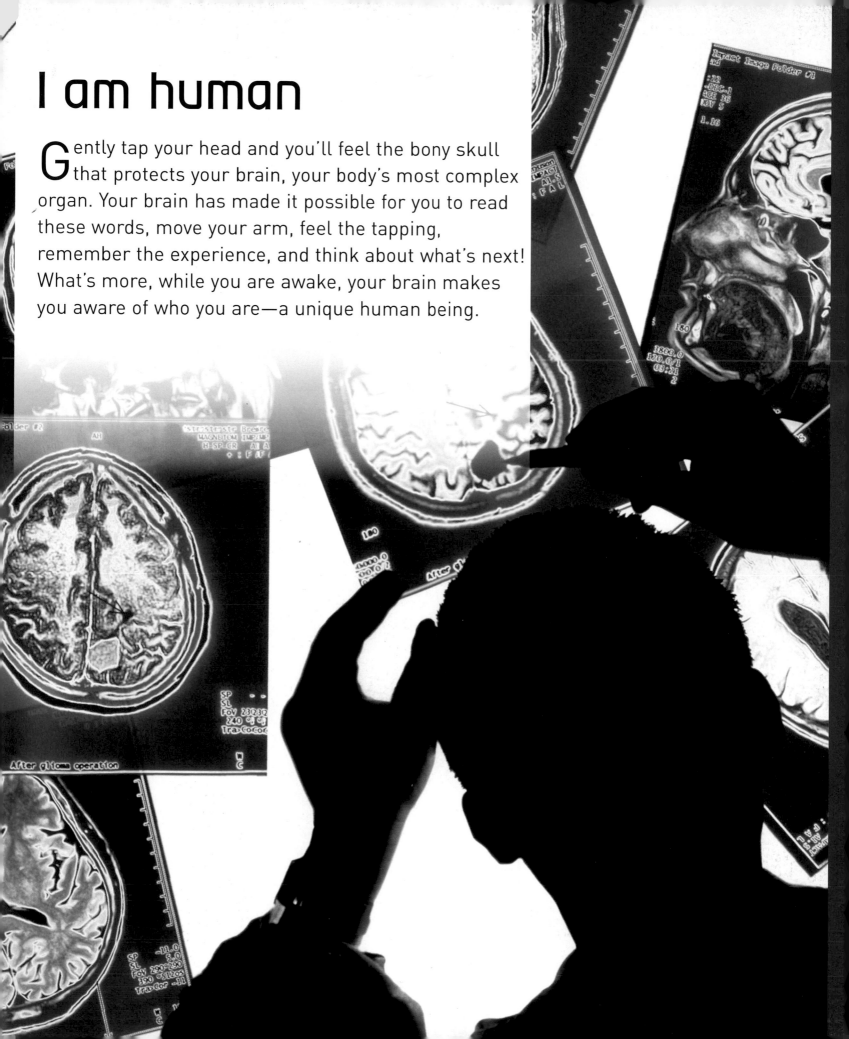

I am human

Gently tap your head and you'll feel the bony skull that protects your brain, your body's most complex organ. Your brain has made it possible for you to read these words, move your arm, feel the tapping, remember the experience, and think about what's next! What's more, while you are awake, your brain makes you aware of who you are—a unique human being.

Controlling and sensing

Almost everything your body does, from taking a breath to thinking up an idea, is controlled by your nervous system. Through receptors inside its sense organs, the nervous system lets you experience the sights, sounds, flavors, and textures of your surroundings.

brain

spinal cord

nervous system

nerve

What is my nervous system?

Your nervous system is made up of your brain, spinal cord, and nerves. This huge control and communication network extends to every part of your body. Your brain receives and processes information from sensory receptors and sends out instructions that control and coordinate your body's activities. The spinal cord runs down your back from the brain. It processes some information and also relays signals between your brain and the rest of your body. Together, the brain and spinal cord form the central nervous system (CNS).

How do my nerves work?

Nerves are the "cables" of your nervous system. They extend from the central nervous system (CNS) to the far reaches of your body. Like your brain and spinal cord, your nerves are made of nerve cells called neurons. Electrical signals called nerve impulses zip along these long, thin cells at high speed. Inside nerves, bundles of neurons either carry signals from the body to the CNS or instructions from the CNS to the body.

bundle of neurons inside a nerve

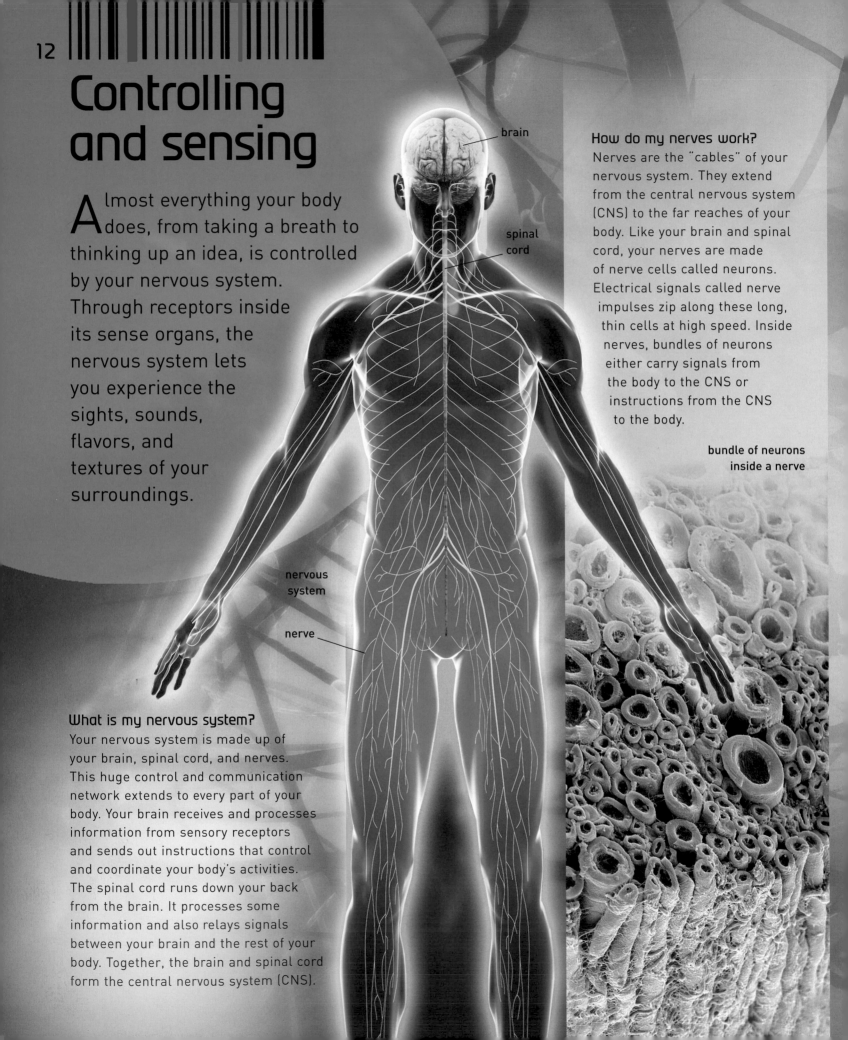

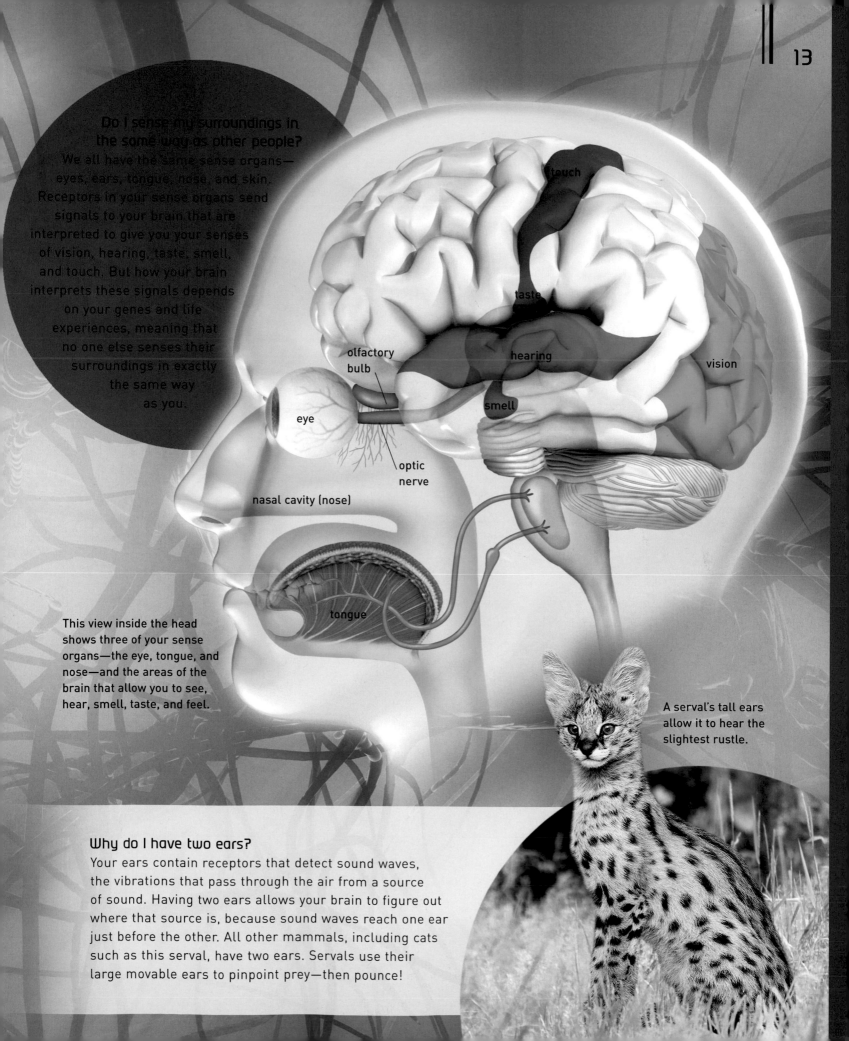

Do I sense my surroundings in the same way as other people?
We all have the same sense organs—eyes, ears, tongue, nose, and skin. Receptors in your sense organs send signals to your brain that are interpreted to give you your senses of vision, hearing, taste, smell, and touch. But how your brain interprets these signals depends on your genes and life experiences, meaning that no one else senses their surroundings in exactly the same way as you.

touch

taste

hearing

vision

olfactory
bulb

smell

eye

optic
nerve

nasal cavity (nose)

tongue

This view inside the head shows three of your sense organs—the eye, tongue, and nose—and the areas of the brain that allow you to see, hear, smell, taste, and feel.

A serval's tall ears allow it to hear the slightest rustle.

Why do I have two ears?
Your ears contain receptors that detect sound waves, the vibrations that pass through the air from a source of sound. Having two ears allows your brain to figure out where that source is, because sound waves reach one ear just before the other. All other mammals, including cats such as this serval, have two ears. Servals use their large movable ears to pinpoint prey—then pounce!

Brainpower

Locked safely inside your skull is a soft, crinkly, and remarkable organ. It is your brain, the most complex living structure in the known universe. Right now, brainpower is allowing you to read these words—but it can do so much more!

Your greedy brain consumes 20 percent of your body's energy but makes up only two percent of your weight.

How does my brain work?

Your brain contains around 100 billion nerve cells called neurons that make and send electrical nerve impulses. Each neuron is connected to thousands of others. This huge network of neurons, buzzing constantly with trillions of electrical and chemical signals, is what gives your brain its brainpower. The neurons' connections allow you to learn, remember, and change.

What does my brain do?

Your brain enables you to think, have a personality, move, sense your surroundings—and a lot more! The left side of the brain controls the right side of the body and, in most people, deals with speech, language, and math skills. The right half controls the left side of the body and usually deals with creativity, face recognition, and spatial awareness. However, there's still plenty to discover about how the brain works.

a network of brain neurons

right   left

Which part of my brain moves my arms?

The biggest part of your brain, the cerebrum, does many different tasks, such as creating feelings, thoughts, and actions. Different areas of the cerebrum have their own jobs to do, as you can see on the brain "map" opposite, but they also work together. To move your arms, the motor (movement) area of your cerebrum sends signals along nerves to arm-moving muscles. A smaller part of your brain, the cerebellum, ensures that those movements are coordinated.

Reading involves different areas of your brain working together.

What is gray matter?

Gray matter is the brain tissue that makes up your cerebral cortex, the thin outer layer of the cerebrum. Gray matter is packed with neurons that help carry out the tasks shown on this brain "map."

thinking

skilled movement

movement

touch

problem solving

spatial awareness

feelings

CEREBRUM

understanding language

hearing

interpreting sound

making images

memory

recognition

CEREBELLUM

coordination and balance

How can doctors check if my brain is working correctly?

To "see" inside your head, doctors can use a range of scanning methods. CAT, MRI, and other scans produce images of the living brain. MRI scans reveal the brain's structure and show any unhealthy tissue.

Your brain processes information received from inside and outside the body and sends out instructions.

MRI scan

Exploring the brain

People have been exploring the brain for thousands of years, trying to discover how it works and which part of it does what. Scientists have an ever-expanding toolbox to investigate brain functions—but your brain still contains many secrets that have not yet been unlocked.

phrenology head showing different "personality areas"

REAL AND RELIGIOUS SENTIMENTS

INTUITIVE,
REASONING, REFLECTIVE,
FACULTIES.

LITERARY,
OBSERVING, KNOWING,
FACULTIES.

PERFECTING GROUP.

PHRENOLOGY

What was phrenology?

Phrenology involved feeling the bumps on a person's skull to determine his or her personality and mental abilities. It was devised by German doctor Franz Gall and was popular in the 1800s. Gall's reasoning was that each brain area related to a feature of the personality. The stronger the feature, the more its brain part should make the skull bulge. Gall's idea turned out to be nonsense—but it established the idea that each brain area has a role.

On this human figure, the parts of the body have been resized in proportion to how much of the brain is involved in controlling their movements.

Who produced the first brain map?

In the 1950s, Canadian brain surgeon Wilder Penfield found that stimulating different parts of his patients' exposed brains made them move or feel sensations. He used these findings to map the brain. Penfield also showed that there are differences in the sizes of the brain areas devoted to each body part.

shoulder
torso
elbow
hip knee
wrist
hand
ankle
fingers
toes
neck
eyes
face
lips

tongue

This slice through the brain shows which areas control the movement of which body parts.

Can scientists "see" my brain in action?

Some scanning techniques such as fMRI (functional magnetic resonance imaging) allow scientists and doctors to "see" and record brain activity as it happens in a living patient. These scans can show which part of your brain is responsible for a particular action or sensation.

fMRI scan showing the area (red) of the brain's right side that controls left-hand movement

colored neurons from a "brainbow" mouse's brain

What is a "brainbow" mouse?

A brainbow mouse is a mouse that has had some of its genes altered so that its brain neurons glow in a wide range of colors. This clever technique allows scientists to create a detailed map of the "wiring" inside the mouse's brain.

Me, myself

Every time you look in a mirror, you see someone you clearly know. Yourself! And you are not only seeing your face reflected there but also your personality—your self-image, self-awareness, and even your private thoughts. Together, they give you consciousness and a unique experience of life.

Why do I daydream?

Daydreaming gives you the chance to take time out. You can think about and picture things you really want to do and imagine that they're going to happen. We enjoy our daydreams, but they serve a useful purpose, too—they help motivate us.

What is consciousness?

No one fully understands consciousness, but we think that it is unique to humans. While you are awake, consciousness gives you an awareness of self, knowledge of who you are, and the ability to focus on both the outside world and your private, inner world. Consciousness includes your thoughts, plans, ideas, feelings, sensations, imagination, and daydreams. No single part of your brain creates consciousness—it depends on activity throughout your whole brain.

Where did my personality come from?

Your personality is unique to you and is determined by your genes and your upbringing. Scientists have come up with all sorts of ways to try to "measure" personality. The five-point test focuses on five characteristics: how organized you are, how outgoing you are, your sensitivity, how easy you are to get along with, and how open you are to new experiences. In reality, of course, your personality is much too complex to be pinned down by looking at only five of its features!

Will my personality change as I get older?

Changes in the way you feel and react to others do happen, especially during the teenage years. Recent research using brain scans shows that the network of connections between brain cells that you lay down in childhood is "pruned" during adolescence in order to make your brain work more efficiently. Side effects of this pruning can include moodiness and fatigue.

What makes someone left-handed?

The brain's cerebrum is split into linked left and right halves, each controlling the opposite side of the body. In 90 percent of people, the left half dominates, so they are right-handed. The remaining ten percent are left-handed. Handedness is determined by genes.

I remember

Memory is how you store all of your experiences and knowledge, and it makes you who you are. Without memory, you would not be able to learn, have a sense of time, recall vacations, play music, or recognize your friends and relatives.

procedural memory

Are there different types of memory?

Yes. Short-term memory, such as remembering a phone number long enough to dial it, lasts only seconds or minutes. Long-term memory can last for years and has three forms. Episodic memory deals with significant events, such as winning a competition. Semantic memory is concerned with facts and knowledge. Procedural memory stores skills, such as the ability to play an instrument.

episodic memory

semantic memory

London taxi drivers memorize hundreds of routes and landmarks. They often have a larger-than-average hippocampus.

Where are memories stored?

Long-term memories are laid down when the brain's hippocampus "plays back" experiences to the areas of the cerebral cortex that first detected them—for example, the visual or hearing areas. Memories are formed when the connections between neurons are strengthened.

Do some people have photographic memories?

It's possible to develop a photographic memory through training, but for people like British artist Stephen Wiltshire, it comes naturally. Stephen has autism, a condition that makes communication and relationships difficult, but he also has an amazing ability. He can accurately draw buildings and cityscapes from memory after seeing them only briefly.

drawing the New York City skyline from memory

The Globe of London
by Stephen Wiltshire
(b. 1974)

Do elephants really never forget?

Research on African elephants has shown that they do have good memories, especially the matriarch—the older female that leads the herd. Using memories of sight, sound, and smell, she can identify whether new arrivals are old friends or possible enemies. There is even some evidence that elephants visit "elephant graveyards." This elephant is touching the skull of a dead ancestor with her trunk.

Learning and thinking

Being able to learn and think is what makes you one of the smartest animals on the planet. Gaining skills depends on effort, experience, practice, and memory. Thinking allows you to create, imagine, reason, make decisions, and solve problems.

It takes time to learn how to ride a bicycle.

When did I learn the most?

Your most intensive period of learning was when you were a small child. In only a few years, you learned to walk, run, talk, read, write, and so much more. When you are young, your brain is constantly rewiring itself, laying down memory circuits so that you don't forget what you've learned.

Why is practice important?

Whether you're learning to ride a bike or play a computer game, practice is vital. Through a process of trial and error, you build on success and avoid repeating mistakes so that you gradually get better. Repetition also reinforces the memory circuits in your brain that store particular skills.

Do I learn by copying?

As a child, you're programmed to acquire skills by watching your parents or other adults and imitating what they do. You learn to brush your teeth by copying what your mom or dad does, for example. Pretend play and make-believe often involve copying and practicing skills that you'll need when you are older.

A little girl copies her dad.

What is lateral thinking?

Sometimes, the only way to solve a difficult problem is to think "outside the box" rather than taking the most obvious approach. This technique, called lateral thinking, involves thinking in a creative way that's a little different. See if you can use lateral thinking to solve the puzzle below.

Copy these dots onto paper. Link all of the dots using four straight lines, without lifting the pen off the paper or going over a line more than once.

Solution on page 30.

Put into words

All animals communicate, but humans are the only animals that communicate using spoken language. Your brain chooses words that reflect your experiences, feelings, actions, or ideas. When you say these words, other people can hear them and understand what you mean.

How did I learn to speak?

When you were born, your brain was already "hard-wired" to recognize and learn language. From around six months old, you babbled many sounds. By listening to the speech of the people around you, you began to understand particular words. Soon, you were forming those words for yourself and, eventually, stringing them together into sentences.

What's my voice box?

Your larynx, or voice box, is located below your throat. Stretched across it are two membranes called vocal cords that work with your breathing system to give you your voice. When your vocal cords tighten, bursts of air make them vibrate and create sounds that your tongue and lips turn into speech.

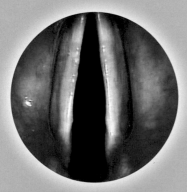

Vocal cords open during breathing.

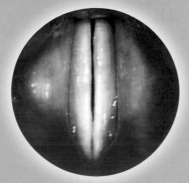

Vocal cords tighten during speaking.

Hello? Can you hear me?

What is Broca's area?

Broca's area is one part of your brain that is involved in speech and writing. It was discovered by a 19th-century French doctor, Paul Broca, who had a patient who could say only one word. When the patient died, Broca examined his brain and found a damaged area on the left side. Broca concluded that this area was needed to produce language.

Why is it that I can talk but chimps can't?

In both humans and chimps, a gene called FOXP2 regulates other genes that help control brain and head development. The human version of FOXP2 creates the brain "wiring" and jaw and throat shapes that enable you to speak. The chimp version doesn't do that. This could be part of the reason why chimps can produce sounds but not speech.

This MRI scan shows activity in Broca's area during speech.

Ooh! Ooh! Ooh!

Is my voice unique?

Yes. Your voice is unique because it depends on the specific shapes and movements of your vocal cords, throat, tongue, and lips. Together, they produce the waves of sound that travel through the air for others to hear. A "voiceprint" (above) is an image that shows the "shape" of these sounds—and no one else has a voiceprint exactly the same as yours.

How brainy?

Humans are the smartest creatures on Earth. Your intelligence depends on the skills and abilities you use to learn, think, reason, and solve problems. Intelligence is also involved in being imaginative and creative and affects how you interact with others and your surroundings.

Albert Einstein

Does intelligence depend on brain size?

When genius physicist Albert Einstein died in 1955, his brain was found to be average. There doesn't seem to be a link between intelligence and brain size. However, people with higher IQs are thought to have more brain neurons with more connections between them, larger brain areas that deal with reasoning, and faster nerve impulses.

Are there different types of intelligence?

People vary in their skills and abilities, so there are different types of intelligence. You may be good at music or have a special understanding of math and logic. Perhaps you excel at languages or you may be a budding naturalist, getting to grips with your surroundings. You may possess excellent movement skills or strong spatial awareness. There are also forms of emotional intelligence—being good at understanding others or understanding yourself.

Can intelligence be measured?

It is almost impossible to sum up intelligence, but that hasn't stopped scientists from trying! One measure is intelligence quotient, or IQ. It is determined by assessing a person's math, verbal, reasoning, and spatial skills. IQ compares someone's mental age with his or her actual age. Most people score between 70 and 130. However, IQ is controversial because it ignores many aspects of intelligence, such as interpersonal skills.

an intelligence test from the 1930s

children at a school in Malawi, southeast Africa

Why do I have to go to school?

Intelligence is not only determined by the genes you inherit from your parents. As you grow, outside influences help you develop your skills and abilities. A big influence during childhood is going to school. There, you learn to read and write. You come into contact with inspiring teachers and discover new subjects. Very importantly, you meet other children, and that helps you develop, too.

Can I increase my intelligence?

Entire countries have seen increases in average IQ over the past 100 years because of improvements in education, diet, and other environmental factors. There is also evidence that brain-stretching puzzles and games, such as chess, increase aspects of your intelligence. This provides further evidence that your surroundings and upbringing have an impact on your intelligence and that working harder in a more stimulating environment can boost your IQ.

Sweet dreams

You spend as much as one third of your life asleep, but this time is not wasted. Sleep allows your body to rest, and it may also give your brain time to sort out the day's experiences and file them away in your memory.

A patient's brain waves are measured as she sleeps.

What is my sleep cycle?

When you're asleep, your brain goes through cycles of activity. A phase of deep sleep, with lower brain activity, is followed by lighter REM (rapid eye movement) sleep, when the brain is busier and dreaming occurs. This pattern is repeated every 90 minutes.

Does my brain stop working when I'm asleep?

Your brain still works, but its activity changes. For one thing, it no longer needs to keep track of your surroundings in the same way. We know the brain is active because its neurons create a "chatter" of electrical signals that can be detected as brain waves.

A baby sleeps 16 hours a day.

An adult sleeps 8 hours a day.

An older adult sleeps 6 hours a day.

Why do I have dreams?

There are many theories about why people dream, but no one truly knows. The most popular explanation is that dreams are created as the sleeping brain sorts through the day's events and sends some to be stored as memories. Whatever their cause, dreams let you experience stories that can be exciting or dull, joyous or terrifying—and some that make no sense at all!

How do dolphins sleep and swim at the same time?

Dolphins never fall fast asleep —if they did, they wouldn't be able to keep an eye out for predators. Instead, they let only half of their brain sleep at a time, leaving the other half fully conscious. Then, every so often, they switch sides.

Why do some people sleepwalk?

During deep sleep, most people move around in bed. But a few actually get up and sleepwalk. Some even go to the kitchen and raid the fridge! Sleepwalkers are not acting out dreams, because during dream (REM) sleep, the body doesn't move. They are sleepwalking because, oddly, their brain is half asleep and half awake.

Brain trainers
See how well your amazing
brain absorbed the facts in Chapter 1.

1. Your brain contains one billion neurons
(nerve cells). True or false?

2. Unscramble PHONE GLORY to find
a nonsensical way of discovering
someone's personality.

3. We sometimes measure
intelligence using:
a) IT   b) ID   c) IQ

Answers on
page 90.

Did you know?
• Between them, your two
eyes house 70 percent of your
body's sensory receptors.

• You can detect 20,000 different smells
but only five tastes—sweet, sour, salty,
bitter, and umami (savory). Chilies
"taste" hot because they
trigger pain receptors
on your tongue.

Lateral thinking
Did you come up with a solution
to the puzzle on page 23? The trick is
to go beyond the boundaries of the "box."
Here's one possible solution:

Conscientious or
disorganized?
Whether you're neat and fussy
(conscientious) or messy and a
chore hater (disorganized) is only one
aspect of your personality.

1. When I start reading a book, I:
a) usually finish reading it,
even if it's hard going
b) sometimes put it to one side
c) usually give up after
a few pages

Continued on page 50.

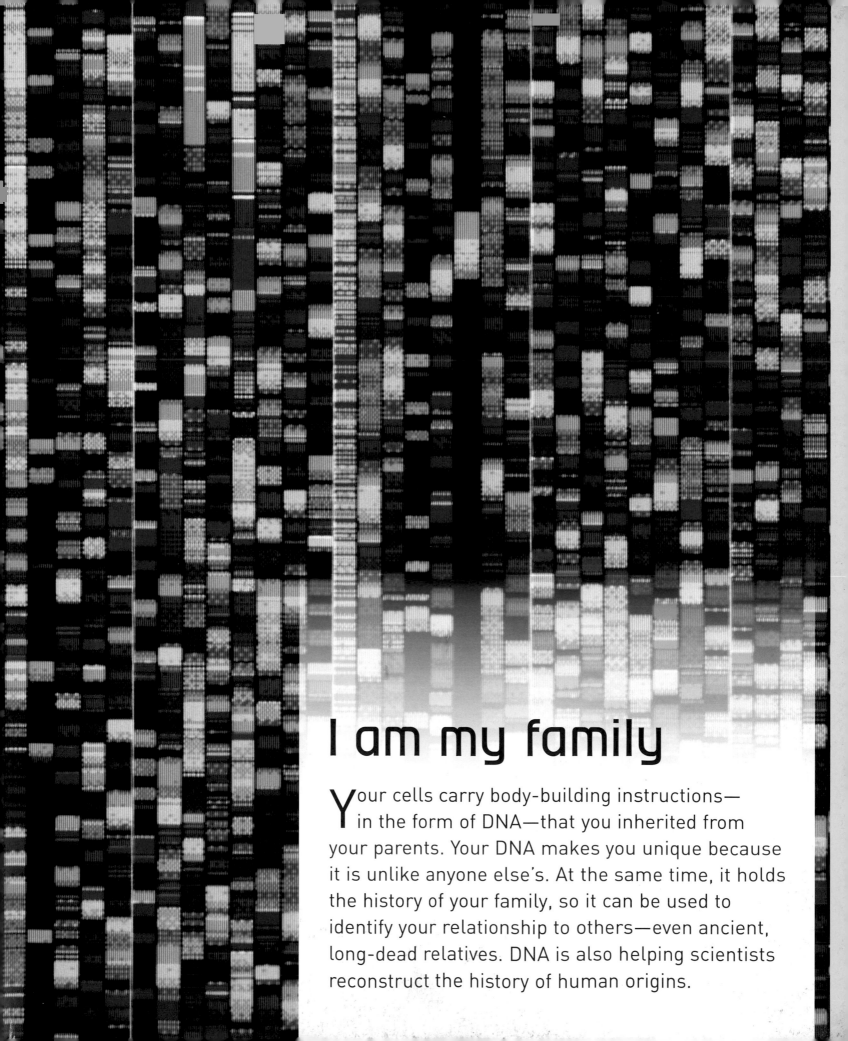

I am my family

Your cells carry body-building instructions— in the form of DNA—that you inherited from your parents. Your DNA makes you unique because it is unlike anyone else's. At the same time, it holds the history of your family, so it can be used to identify your relationship to others—even ancient, long-dead relatives. DNA is also helping scientists reconstruct the history of human origins.

My cells

...thing you are made from micro... ...tiny structures and che... ...body... are organized into ti... ...organs, ...to a working human bo... ...this ...you would be a shape...

A tiger's body contains around 200 trillion cells.

How many cells does it take to make me?

It takes trillions! We start life as a single cell that divides repeatedly to produce, eventually, the 100 trillion (million million) cells in an adult's body. Being made of many cells is something we share with most other living things. Some life forms, however, such as some bacteria, are made up of only one cell.

The nucleus is surrounded by the nuclear membrane.

Chromosomes contain the instructions to run the cell.

Mitochondria release energy.

Ribosomes help make proteins.

What's inside my cells?

Cells are very tiny and can be seen only by using a microscope (right). Very powerful microscopes reveal that cells have a complex structure, as the artwork (above right) of a "typical" cell shows. Each cell has an outer cell membrane and an inner control center, the nucleus. Jellylike cytoplasm, which fills the rest of the cell, contains many minute structures, such as mitochondria, that work together so that the cell can survive, perform its tasks, and grow.

neuron (nerve cell)

Are all of my cells the same?

There are around 200 different types of body cells. Nerve cells, or neurons, form your brain and nerves and carry signals at high speed (see page 12). Fat cells store energy and keep you warm. Muscle cells make you move. Red blood cells deliver oxygen around the body. The shape, size, and features of each cell type relate to its specific job. But most cells share the same structure and workings (see below left).

adipose (fat) cells

The cell membrane controls what enters and leaves the cell.

The cytoplasm consists of jellylike fluid.

skeletal muscle cells

dead, worn-away skin cells

How long do my cells live?

Each type of body cell has a different life span. Brain cells can last a lifetime, while skin cells can last only a few weeks. By the time you have read this sentence, 50 million of your cells will have been replaced.

What are tissues and organs?

Cells of the same type, such as liver cells, work together as a tissue. Two or more types of tissues make up an organ, such as the liver, which "cleans" the blood. Other organs include the brain and kidneys. Linked organs form a body system, such as the digestive system.

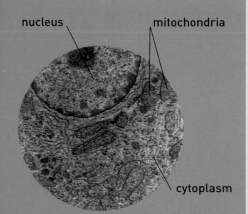

nucleus   mitochondria

cytoplasm

inside a liver cell

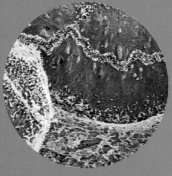

liver tissue

liver (organ)

Chromosomes in control

A lmost all of your body cells contain chromosomes. These microscopic structures store your genes—the instructions that control your cells' activities. When cells divide, so that your body can grow or repair itself, chromosomes are passed on to the new cells.

Where exactly are my chromosomes?

Long, threadlike chromosomes are packed inside each body cell's nucleus. Every strand consists of a substance called DNA that, uniquely, can copy itself. During cell division, chromosomes shorten and duplicate themselves to form two linked strands. Then the strands pull apart so that the two "offspring" cells have identical chromosomes.

1. The chromosomes shorten.
2. Copied chromosomes form X shapes.
3. The chromosomes line up.
4. The linked strands separate.
5. The cell starts to split in half.
6. Two identical "offspring" cells form.

How many chromosomes do I have?

Your cells contain two sets of 23 chromosomes—that is, 46 in all. One set comes from your mother (maternal) and one from your father (paternal). This picture taken with a microscope shows a person's 23 pairs of chromosomes arranged in order of size from the longest to the shortest. The 23rd pair is the sex chromosomes (see pages 43 and 64–65), in this case XX (female). XY is male.

What are genes?

Genes are the instructions needed to build and run your cells and, therefore, your body. Genes influence not only the appearance and workings of the body but also your health, personality, and much, much more. Each chromosome is made up of a long DNA molecule, and each gene instruction consists of one short section of this molecule. One set of chromosomes carries around 23,000 genes.

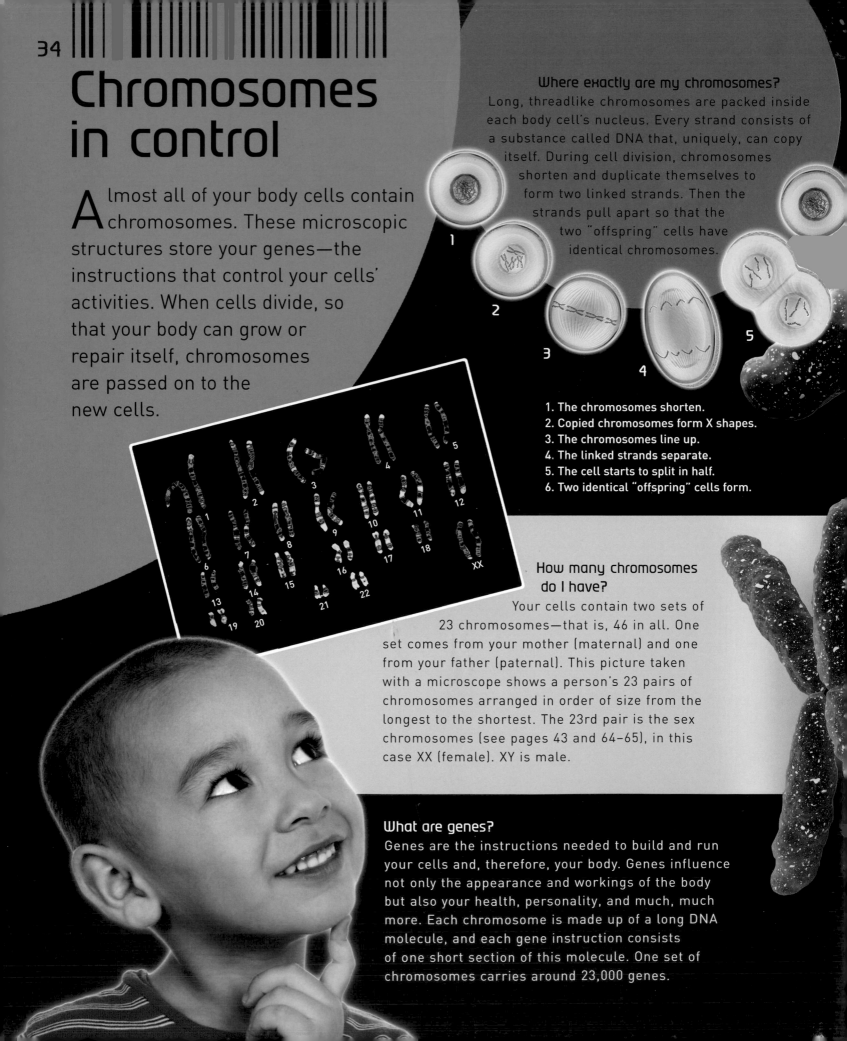

Are my genes like everyone else's?
Your genes are the same as
everyone else's—that's what makes
you human. But these genes may
have different versions called alleles—
that's what makes you an individual. For
example, if you can't see an eye shape in this
sight test (right), you have an allele that makes
you unable to tell red from green. If you can see
the eye, you have a different allele that allows you
to tell red from green.

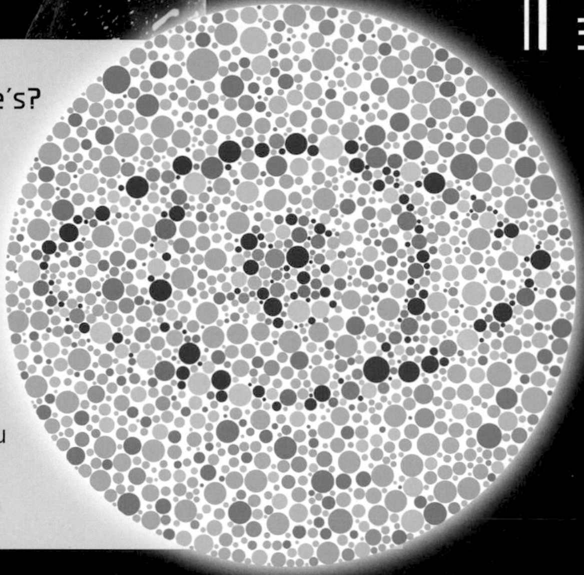

6

A chimp's 48 chromosomes
carry genes very
similar to yours.

Chromosomes look X shaped
during cell division because
they have copied themselves
into two strands.

**How similar
am I to a
chimpanzee?**
Your genes are 98
percent similar to those
found in chimpanzees,
making chimps your
closest relatives. However,
you also share 50 percent of
your genes with bananas, which
suggests that all living things
work in the same basic way.

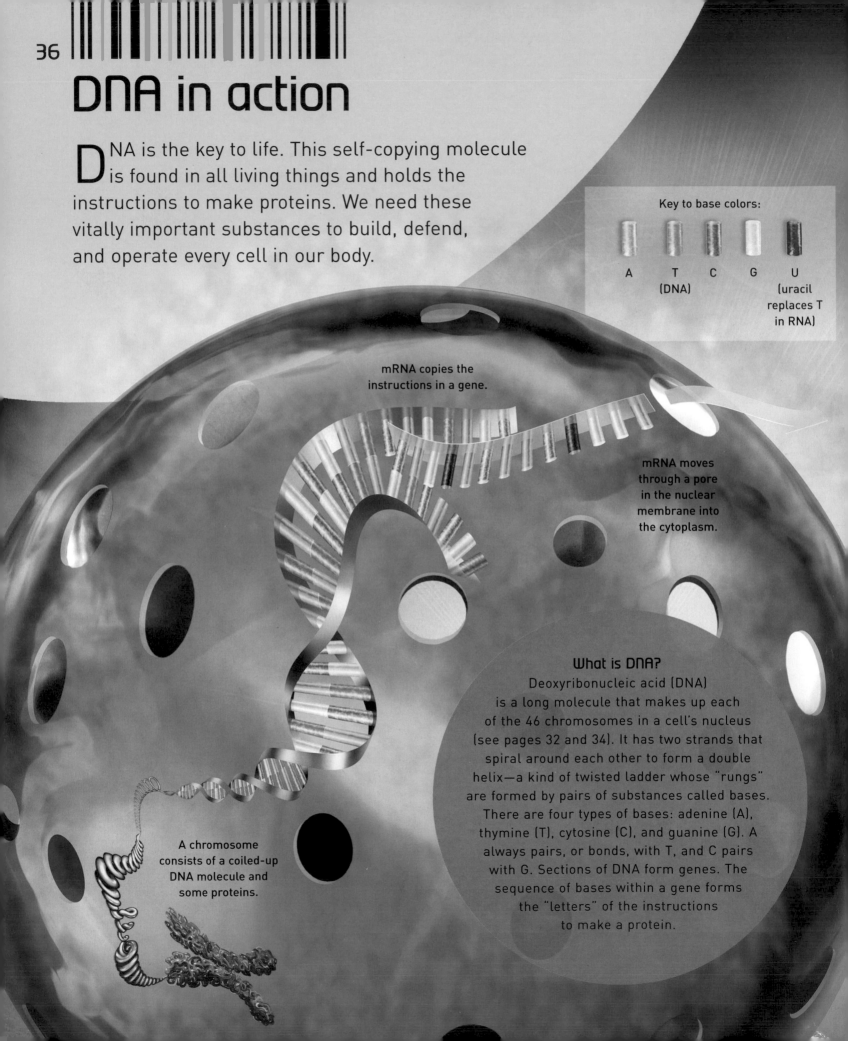

DNA in action

DNA is the key to life. This self-copying molecule is found in all living things and holds the instructions to make proteins. We need these vitally important substances to build, defend, and operate every cell in our body.

Key to base colors:

A   T   C   G   U
    (DNA)   (uracil
                replaces T
                in RNA)

mRNA copies the instructions in a gene.

mRNA moves through a pore in the nuclear membrane into the cytoplasm.

A chromosome consists of a coiled-up DNA molecule and some proteins.

What is DNA?

Deoxyribonucleic acid (DNA) is a long molecule that makes up each of the 46 chromosomes in a cell's nucleus (see pages 32 and 34). It has two strands that spiral around each other to form a double helix—a kind of twisted ladder whose "rungs" are formed by pairs of substances called bases. There are four types of bases: adenine (A), thymine (T), cytosine (C), and guanine (G). A always pairs, or bonds, with T, and C pairs with G. Sections of DNA form genes. The sequence of bases within a gene forms the "letters" of the instructions to make a protein.

How are my proteins made?

Proteins are made in the cytoplasm of a cell. However, DNA cannot leave the cell nucleus. Instead, it "unzips" so that the bases on one strand can be copied by messenger RNA (mRNA). Then the mRNA moves into the cytoplasm and attaches to a ribosome. Transfer RNA (tRNA) molecules arrive, each carrying an amino acid. Each tRNA bonds to the "right" bases on mRNA, leaving behind an amino acid that joins the growing protein chain.

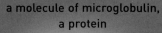

a molecule of microglobulin, a protein

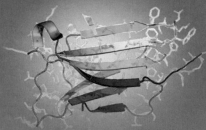

The chain of amino acids will form a protein molecule.

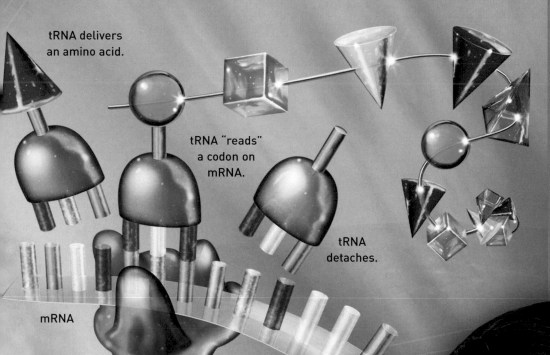

tRNA delivers an amino acid.

tRNA "reads" a codon on mRNA.

tRNA detaches.

mRNA

ribosome

Why are proteins so important?

There are thousands of proteins in your body, and they do many different jobs. Some proteins build or support your cells. Microglobulin, for example, forms part of the cell membrane (wall). Proteins also include hormones, oxygen-carrying hemoglobin, and the antibodies that protect you from infections. Enzymes, the substances that control the chemical reactions that keep your cells alive, are proteins, too.

What is the genetic code?

The genetic code is what cells use to turn bases carried on mRNA into the chain of amino acids that make up a specific protein. The genetic code uses "words" that are three bases long called codons. Each codon on mRNA specifies which of the 20 types of amino acids should be delivered by tRNA and lined up to join the growing protein molecule.

Unraveling the genome

Your genome is all of the DNA in your body's cells. In 1990, the international Human Genome Project embarked on a mission to unravel our genome and decode our genes. It was completed only 50 years after the discovery of DNA's structure.

Rosalind Franklin

When was DNA's structure discovered?
Scientists first thought that DNA carried genetic information in the 1940s. But it wasn't until 1953 that James Watson and Francis Crick, helped by data from fellow scientist Rosalind Franklin, constructed a model that revealed the structure of a DNA molecule (see page 36).

James Watson (left) and Francis Crick

1869 Johann Miescher isolates "nuclein" (DNA).

1944 Scientists believe that genes are carried by DNA.

1953 The structure of the DNA molecule is discovered.

1965 The complete DNA genetic code is deciphered.

2003 The HGP finishes sequencing the human genome.

What did the Human Genome Project do?

DNA is made up of a sequence of four bases, represented by the letters A, T, C, and G (see page 36). The Human Genome Project (HGP) set out to record the order of these bases, including those that spell out the coded instructions in genes. HGP scientists cut up human DNA into overlapping pieces, "read" the sequence of bases, and then used computers to reconstruct the order of bases in whole chromosomes. Completed in 2003, the HGP showed that the human genome contains 3.2 billion base pairs.

sample of human DNA

Have other genomes been sequenced?

Scientists have now sequenced the genomes for hundreds of other life forms, including the chimpanzee, cat, mouse, zebra fish, fruit fly, roundworm, yeast (a fungus), and many bacteria. Comparing genomes shows how closely related organisms are and provides clues about the effects of genes.

fruit fly

What is "junk DNA"?

The HGP showed that genes, which contain coded instructions to make proteins (see page 37), make up hardly any of the genome. Almost all of it consists of noncoding DNA, originally called "junk DNA" because it was believed to be meaningless and useless. Now, however, scientists have found that some noncoding DNA can control genes. Other sections include genes that no longer work, the remains of viruses that infected our ancestors, and repeated sequences of bases that are used in DNA profiling (see pages 40–41).

mouse "baldness" caused by a mutant gene

What makes my genome unique?

Any two people's genomes differ by around one base in every thousand. These differences result from mistakes in the copying of DNA during cell division—the mistakes cause mutations (changes) in the base sequence. Outside factors, such as chemicals, can also cause mutations. Most mutations occur in noncoding DNA, but some affect genes, with harmful (see pages 80–81), beneficial, or no effects. The 1000 Genomes Project, launched in 2008, is comparing the DNA sequence of people worldwide.

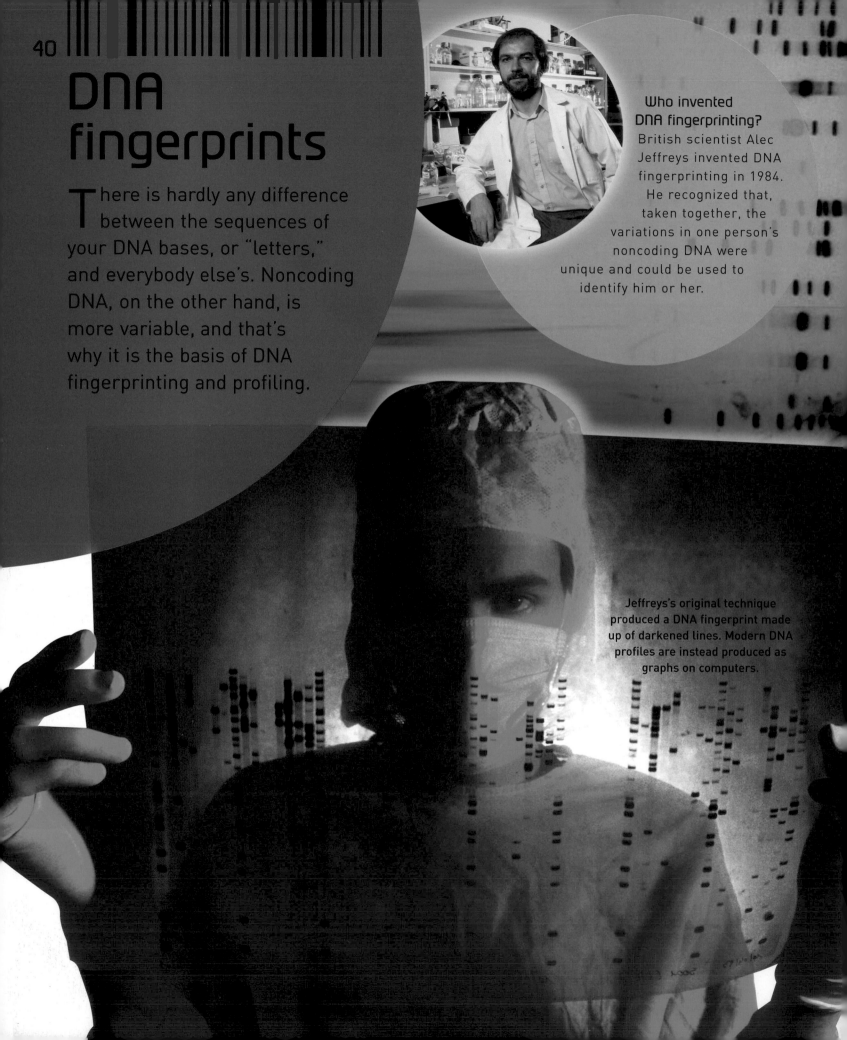

DNA fingerprints

There is hardly any difference between the sequences of your DNA bases, or "letters," and everybody else's. Noncoding DNA, on the other hand, is more variable, and that's why it is the basis of DNA fingerprinting and profiling.

Who invented DNA fingerprinting? British scientist Alec Jeffreys invented DNA fingerprinting in 1984. He recognized that, taken together, the variations in one person's noncoding DNA were unique and could be used to identify him or her.

Jeffreys's original technique produced a DNA fingerprint made up of darkened lines. Modern DNA profiles are instead produced as graphs on computers.

Can DNA fingerprinting catch criminals?

Everyone's fingertips have a unique pattern. You leave an oily copy of this pattern behind, in the form of a fingerprint, when you touch something. If you leave prints at a crime scene, they prove you were there. Everyone's DNA profile is unique, too. Only a few cells can be enough to make a DNA profile. Investigators compare DNA profiles produced from samples taken at the scene of a crime with ones taken from suspects to confirm or rule out their guilt.

The crime scene

1. Skin cells flake off the body and are left behind through touch.
2. Saliva left on half-eaten food or used cups may contain cells from the lining of a criminal's mouth.
3. A bloody fingerprint on a tissue contains white blood cells.
4. Roots of any hairs left at the crime scene contain living cells.
5. A forensic scientist examines samples from the crime scene.
6. The scientist transfers a cell sample into a tube for analysis.

Family ties

Y ou've seen how DNA profiling or fingerprinting is useful for solving crimes. But it can also be used to find answers to other mysteries—to check whether people are related to each other or to help you trace your ancestors.

Just how alike are we?
We may look different, but we are very alike in terms of DNA. In any two people, 99.9 percent (99.95 percent in close relatives) of the DNA base sequences in their genomes are identical. The remaining 0.1 percent of bases—around three million in all, found mostly in noncoding DNA—vary and can be compared by DNA profiling to test how closely people are related.

Me!

Mom

Dad

Granddad and Grandma

Nana

Grandpa

Granddad's parents

Grandma's parents

Nana's parents

Grandpa's parents

A biological family tree shows the relationships between blood relatives in a family. The girl at the top of the tree inherited one half of her DNA from her father and one half from her mother, as they did from their own parents.

Who's the parent?

Proving that parents and children are related involves comparing DNA profiles, just like a crime scene investigation. A child's chromosomes, inherited from the mother and father, contain sequences of noncoding DNA called short tandem repeats (STRs). The STRs are repeated in patterns unique to that individual. If DNA profiles show that the STRs in the mother's and father's chromosomes match those of the child, they confirm that the parents and child are related.

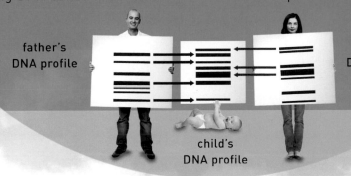

father's DNA profile

mother's DNA profile

child's DNA profile

What is mitochondrial DNA?

Mitochondria are tiny, energy-releasing structures found inside all body cells (see page 32). Unusually, they have their own DNA called mitochondrial DNA, or mtDNA, that passes unchanged from mother to child. People related through female ancestors share the same mtDNA profiles, whereas unrelated people do not. mtDNA profiling provides a powerful tool to track ancestry over many generations (see page 49).

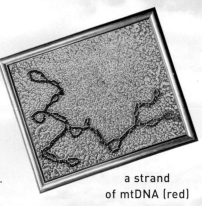

a strand of mtDNA (red)

How do Y chromosomes help us build family trees?

Our 23 pairs of instruction-storing chromosomes (see page 34) include one pair of sex chromosomes, made up of an X and either another X (in females) or a Y (in males). Y chromosomes pass unchanged from father to son, so fathers and sons share the same Y-chromosome DNA profile. In unrelated males, Y-chromosome profiles differ because of variations in noncoding DNA. Y-chromosome profiling is used to trace ancestry and relationships through the male line.

human X (left) and Y (right) sex chromosomes

How does mitochondrial DNA help history come alive?

Since mtDNA can survive for thousands of years, scientists can use it to show relationships between living people and prehistoric ancestors. In 1996, for example, some villagers in Cheddar, U.K., discovered that they were related to Cheddar Man, whose 9,000-year-old skeleton had been found in a local cave. Researchers compared mtDNA from present-day residents of Cheddar with mtDNA from Cheddar Man's teeth and found that some shared a female ancestor with the caveman.

Naming the dead

DNA profiling can identify unknown victims of war, terrorist attacks, and murder by comparing their DNA with that of living relatives. Looking at mitochondrial DNA, or mtDNA, (see page 43) is especially useful because it passes unchanged from mother to child and survives for years in bones and teeth.

New York's Twin Towers collapsing

handling an artifact from a mass grave in Fromelles, France

How did DNA profiling help after 9/11?

On September 11, 2001, a date known as 9/11, terrorists crashed airplanes into the Twin Towers of New York's World Trade Center and killed more than 2,700 people. DNA profiling made it possible to identify many victims of the attack. That meant the remains could be returned to the victims' families and given proper burials.

Australian soldiers before the battle

What's the link between DNA and World War I?

In July 1916, the Battle of Fromelles in northern France claimed the lives of more than 2,000 Australian and British soldiers. Many were buried in unmarked mass graves, one of which was discovered and excavated in 2008. The soldiers' remains were identified through artifacts, such as uniform badges, and by comparing mtDNA and Y-chromosome DNA with that of living relatives.

How did mtDNA analysis close a chapter of Russian history?

Following the Russian Revolution in 1917, the czar (emperor) and his family were executed. Their burial site, however, was not found until 1991. Scientists were able to confirm the identity of the czar's wife, Alexandra, and her children by analyzing their mtDNA and comparing it to living members of the same family. It matched that of Prince Philip, the husband of Great Britain's Queen Elizabeth II, whose maternal grandmother was Alexandra's sister.

remains of the Russian royal family

Czar Nicholas II and his family in 1913

American outlaw Jesse James

Did Jesse James really die in 1882?

Outlaw Jesse James was murdered in 1882 . . . or was he? Rumor had it that his death was faked and someone else was buried in his place. In 1995, the body was exhumed. mtDNA samples from the teeth and hair were identical to those taken from descendants of Jesse's sister. So the buried body really was Jesse!

Human evolution

The earliest humans evolved from apelike ancestors in Africa around seven million years ago (mya). They gave rise to a family tree with many branches, dead ends, and a single surviving species—modern humans.

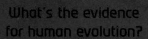

What's the evidence for human evolution?
A paleontologist examines a Homo habilis jawbone, one piece of the evidence for human evolution that comes from fossilized skulls and skeletons. Fossils show that there were more than 20 human species. These fossils also show that humans walked upright and evolved increasingly larger brains.

What does evolution mean?
Evolution is the gradual change that happens over time to all living things. Their unique mix of genes makes certain individuals in a population better suited to their surroundings and more likely to survive and produce offspring than others. This natural selection process, where favored individuals pass on their genes, drives evolution. Over time, new species arise and established species die out. Human evolution has produced many species, some of which are shown here.

2.5–1.8 mya
Homo rudolfensis

3.0–2.0 mya
Australopithecus africanus

2.4–1.5 mya
Homo habilis

3.9–2.9 mya
Australopithecus afarensis

2.3–1.2 mya
Paranthropus boisei

4.5–4.2 mya
Ardipithecus ramidus

How closely related are we to Neanderthals?

The Neanderthals were humans who lived in Eurasia and hunted large prey. We shared a common ancestor around 500,000 years ago. The Neanderthal genome, sequenced in 2010 from DNA extracted from bones that were more than 38,000 years old, shows that we also share more than 99 percent of DNA. What's more, between one and four percent of your genome may come directly from Neanderthals, as a result of breeding between our two species around 45,000 years ago.

Neanderthals had distinctive ridged brow bones.

200,000 ya–present
Homo sapiens

1.8 mya–70,000 ya
Homo erectus

700,000–200,000 ya
Homo heidelbergensis

1.9–1.4 mya
Homo ergaster

230,000–28,000 ya
Homo neanderthalensis
(Neanderthals)

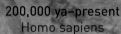

Is human evolution still happening?

Yes, it is. For example, people started herding cattle more than 10,000 years ago. But if they drank their cows' nutritious milk, the herders got sick because they could not digest lactose, the sugar in milk. Around 7,500 years ago, a gene mutation appeared in Europe that allowed adults to digest lactose and drink milk. The mutant gene spread and also arose independently in parts of Africa. But it didn't spread everywhere. More than 70 percent of people in the world cannot drink milk.

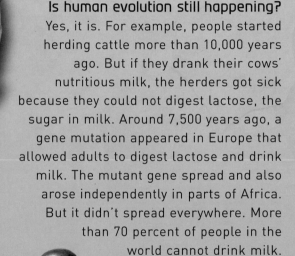

The Masai of East Africa live by raising livestock. Most have the gene that allows them to digest lactose, but a few do not.

Out of Africa

Most scientists agree on two key points about our species, Homo sapiens. First, we—modern humans—evolved in Africa around 200,000 years ago. Second, some humans moved out of Africa about 65,000 years ago and spread around the world.

flow of DNA around the globe

routes of migration

arrival dates

50,000 ya

16,000 ya

EUROPE

ASIA

NORTH AMERICA

EUROPE

40,000 ya

Middle East

50,000 ya

PACIFIC OCEAN

60,000 ya

AFRICA

65,000 ya

Oceania

SOUTH AMERICA

15,000 ya

north

AUSTRALIA

50,000 ya

Where do we come from?

DNA evidence shows that we evolved in Africa and then spread through the Middle East to the Far East, Australia and Oceania, Europe, and the Americas. Isolated by migration, each group of humans acquired unique mutations in their DNA. For example, a DNA mutation common to American Indians shows that their ancestors arrived from Asia 16,000 years ago.

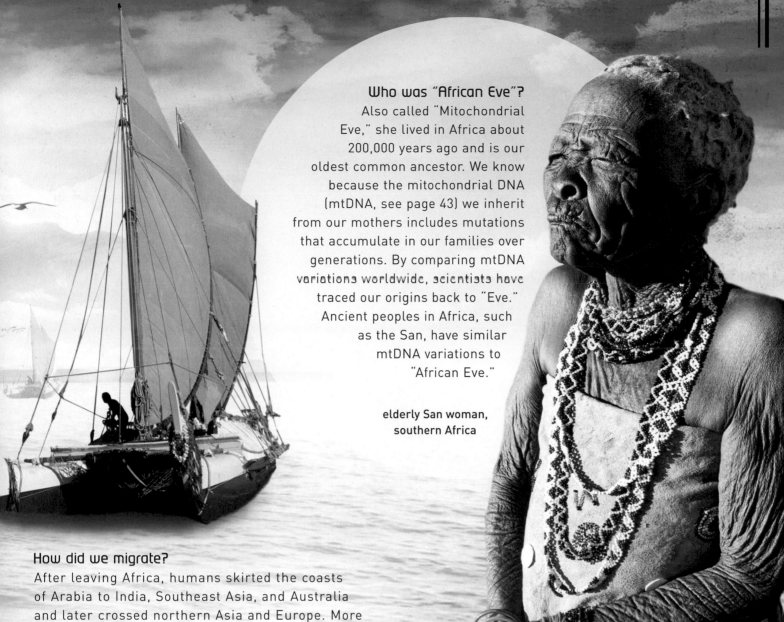

Who was "African Eve"?

Also called "Mitochondrial Eve," she lived in Africa about 200,000 years ago and is our oldest common ancestor. We know because the mitochondrial DNA (mtDNA, see page 43) we inherit from our mothers includes mutations that accumulate in our families over generations. By comparing mtDNA variations worldwide, scientists have traced our origins back to "Eve." Ancient peoples in Africa, such as the San, have similar mtDNA variations to "African Eve."

elderly San woman, southern Africa

How did we migrate?

After leaving Africa, humans skirted the coasts of Arabia to India, Southeast Asia, and Australia and later crossed northern Asia and Europe. More amazing were the sea migrations from Asia to the Pacific islands of Oceania. The *Hokule'a* (above), a recent reconstruction of an ancient voyaging canoe, recreated these voyages without navigational instruments to prove that they were possible.

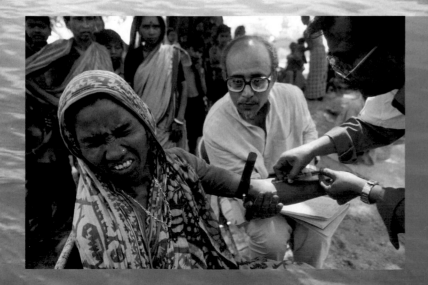

How do we map migration?

A researcher takes a blood sample from an Indian woman to obtain her DNA. This is part of a project being carried out worldwide that looks at mutations in DNA. As bands of people moved from place to place thousands of years ago, mutations occurred in their DNA. These mutations act as markers, because they occurred only in particular populations. Scientists can plot their distribution and then work backward to map migration routes and dates.

Brain trainers
See how well your amazing brain
absorbed the facts in Chapter 2.

1. Who discovered the structure of DNA?

2. Where did humans evolve?
   a) China
   b) America
   c) Africa

3. Unscramble COO HMM SORES to get the
46 structures inside every cell that carry
its building instructions.

Answers
on page 90.

Did you know?
• Stretched out, the DNA from
only one of your cells would extend
for 6 ft. (1.8m).

• Put end to end, the DNA from all of your cells
would reach to the Sun and back 600 times.

• One set of chromosomes inside a body cell
contains about three billion DNA bases.
That's enough "letters" to fill a
pile of paperback books
200 ft. (60m) high.

What can you see?

You can probably see a spiral.
But it doesn't really exist! Your
brain has created it because
the series of circles suggests
that it should be there.

Conscientious or
disorganized?
This personality quiz is
continued from page 30.

2. When I'm doing a school project,
I generally try to:
   a) do my absolute best
   b) put some effort into my work
   c) get things done with as little
   effort as possible

Continued on page 70.

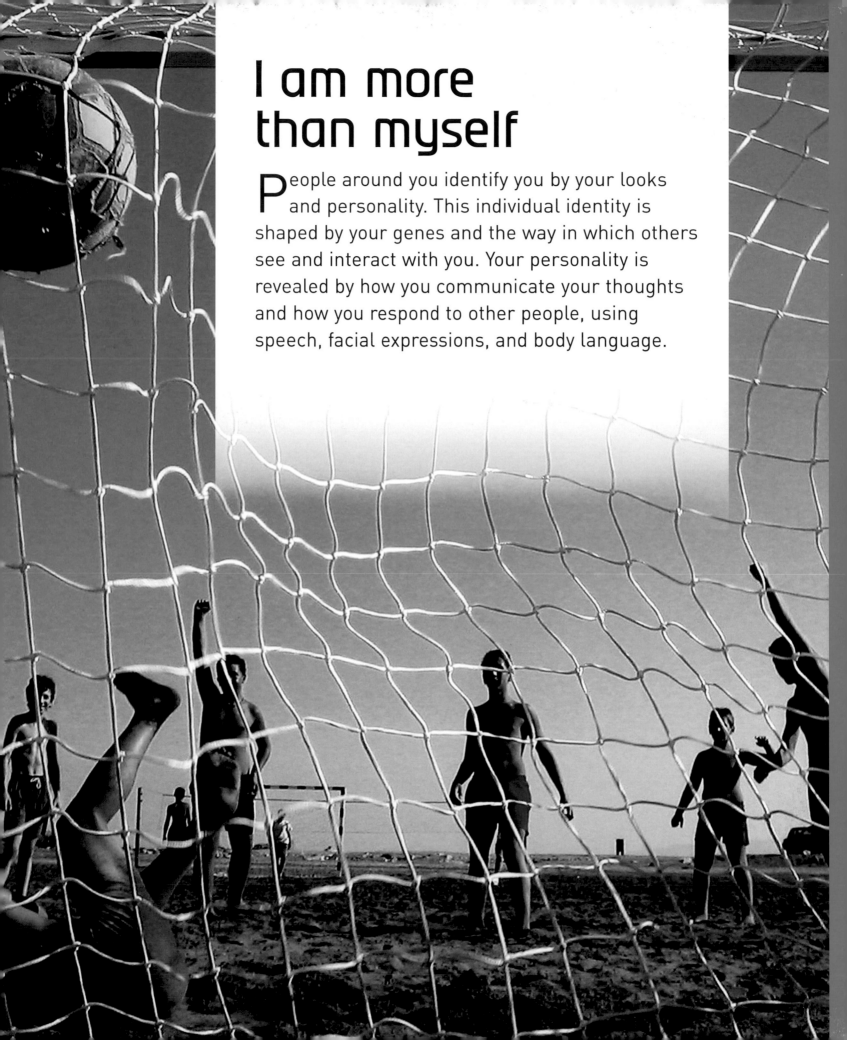

I am more than myself

People around you identify you by your looks and personality. This individual identity is shaped by your genes and the way in which others see and interact with you. Your personality is revealed by how you communicate your thoughts and how you respond to other people, using speech, facial expressions, and body language.

Being sociable

Human beings—all seven billion of us—are social animals. Being able to communicate with others is vital. It allows you to identify yourself and be part of your family and community. You communicate in all sorts of ways, including speech and writing, which are unique to humans.

Hello! Bonjour! Namaste! Ciao!

What is body language?

Without you thinking about it or saying anything, body language communicates your feelings and intentions through your posture, gestures, and facial expressions. It signals whether you are interested or bored, lying or being truthful. Like the young women on this bench (left), you may "mirror" (copy) body language when you are with someone you like.

What is special about speaking?

Whether you shout or whisper, speaking involves saying words in a particular order to create messages that others can understand. You order your words according to rules built into your brain. When talking and listening, you use these strings of words to communicate thoughts, ideas, and opinions, to learn about new things, and to build relationships.

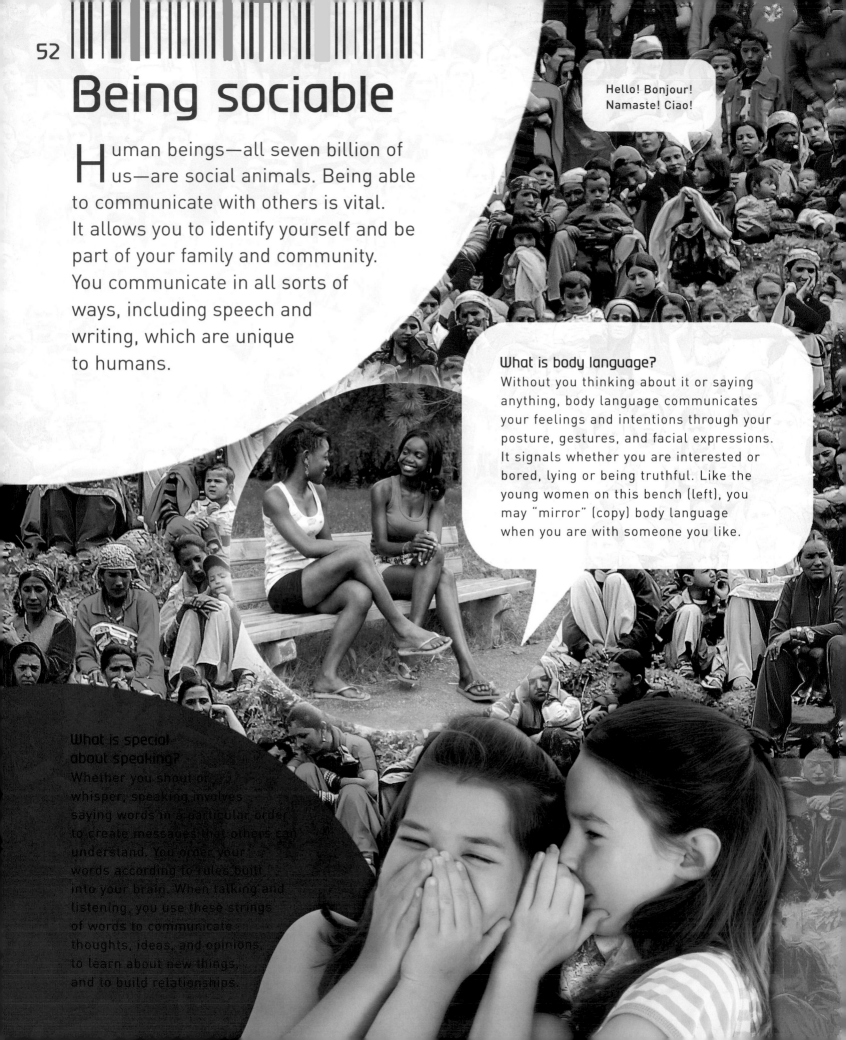

Witaj! Guten Tag! Konnichiwa! ¡Hola! Shalom! Ni hao!

Why are writing and reading so important?

Written language has enabled humans to make amazing cultural and technological progress. It allows us to communicate ideas, memories, and information. These are passed on to future generations, who can build on past discoveries to extend their knowledge. Writing developed about 5,000 years ago as pictures that stood for ideas or objects. These were later simplified into the characters and letters used today.

Sumerian picture writing, c. 3000 B.C.

Worldwide, people speak more than 6,500 different languages. Above are just ten ways to say hello. Find out which languages they are on page 70.

Do other animals talk to one another?

Like us, apes and monkeys are social animals. They communicate through body language, mutual grooming, and making sounds, but unlike humans, they cannot actually talk to one another. As humans evolved from apelike ancestors, talking replaced grooming as a way of bonding and communicating.

mandrills grooming each other

Eyes, nose, and mouth

What's so important about two eyes, a nose, and a mouth? Together, they make up the key features of your face—the part of your body that says the most about you. Incredibly, your face reveals your identity, gender, genetic inheritance, and emotions. It also hints at your age, status, and personality. No wonder we're so fascinated by people's faces!

What determines my eye color?
Whether your eyes are brown, blue, green, hazel, or gray depends on the melanin pigment in your irises. This, in turn, is decided by genes inherited from your parents. If both of your parents are brown-eyed, you and any brothers or sisters are more likely to have brown eyes than any other color.

A digital face-recognition system maps the distances between key points on a grid.

Genes determine the natural color of our eyes—but it's not fixed! Some people wear colored contact lenses to change their eye color.

How does my face affect me?

Faces can be disfigured as a result of genes, disease, or accidents. This doesn't alter who you are, but in a culture obsessed with appearance, it can affect how you are treated. It may make people, wrongly, view you as inferior and less able. It will take time for attitudes to change. In the meantime, some people with facial disfigurement, such as Vicky Lucas (right), who has cherubism, campaign to be treated just like everyone else.

Vicky has cherubism, a rare genetic condition that causes abnormal bone growth.

What's so special about my face?

Your face is unique because of its shape, coloring, and the spacing of its features. It will age and change over time, but the relative positions of your eyes, nose, and mouth will stay the same. Face recognition relies on this. You recognize faces by comparing them to faces stored in your memory (see page 56). Digital face-recognition systems work in a similar way.

Tattoos change facial appearance. They may be part of a person's culture, like this Maori man's swirling patterns. Or they may be a matter of individual choice.

Jewelry, piercings, and makeup can alter or emphasize facial features.

Identifying others

You identify other people around you by recognizing their most memorable feature—their face. Amazingly, your brain is capable of recognizing and remembering up to 10,000 faces.

Which part of my brain recognizes faces?

In most people, the brain's right side recognizes faces. When you look at a face, the brain's visual area processes information from your eyes to produce a basic image. If it includes likely facial features, the image is sent to your brain's face-recognition area to be identified as a face. If it matches other faces held in your memory, you recognize the person it belongs to.

a view of the right side of the brain

visual area

face-recognition area

Why does this boy's face look so odd?

Turn the book upside down and this boy's face might surprise you! Your brain's face-recognition area only processes objects that, from top to bottom, have the expected facial features. An upside-down face is dealt with by a brain area that is not sensitive to face patterns. But turn the image the right way around and your brain's face-recognition area soon tells you that something is not quite right.

What is face blindness?

You can probably make out a face in this portrait by Arcimboldo, an Italian artist who specialized in creating heads from everyday objects. But anyone who has prosopagnosia, or face blindness, will see only fruit and vegetables. In the two percent of people who have face blindness, the brain's face-recognition area does not work properly. They can recognize neither faces—even those of family and friends—nor patterns that suggest faces.

Whimsical Portrait by Giuseppe Arcimboldo (1527–1593)

"criminal" composite by Francis Galton, 1878

Can I judge someone by his or her face?

No, but English scientist Francis Galton (1822–1911) believed he could. He thought that all human attributes, including criminal behavior, were inherited and had nothing to do with other factors, such as upbringing, poverty, or diet. Galton put together composite photos of convicted criminals' faces to try to show which features were a sign of criminal tendencies. He failed to convince anyone, though.

Do babies recognize faces?

One of the ways that a mother and her baby bond is by exchanging facial expressions. But do babies actually recognize their mother's face? Research using paddles (below, left) found that babies spend more time responding to patterns that resemble a face than those that do not. It seems that babies do recognize faces and that facial recognition is already built-in or "hard-wired" into the brain at birth.

paddles to test facial recognition in babies

A mother and baby make eye contact.

Feeling emotional

Emotions are sophisticated responses that help you survive.
They prepare your body to react in rewards. Basic
emotions are ones you feel from joy to surprise.
These include hope, pride, and more complex emotions
such as love, guilt, and shame are shaped by
society and more complex emotions.

Which part of my brain produces emotions?

The limbic system (shown above by the colored areas) works with the surrounding cerebrum to make, recognize, and control emotions. Each part has a job to do. The amygdala (blue), for example, deals with fear, while the cingulate gyrus (pale pink) helps you express your feelings.

Why do I have emotions?

A look of disapproval clearly communicates this girl's feelings. Emotions determine how you feel and behave. They protect you from harm and help you react to all kinds of situations. You display your emotions to others in many ways, including facial expressions and body language (see pages 52–53).

What is empathy?

Empathy is the ability to sympathize with other people and put yourself in their place. Scientists think that this feeling for others depends on brain cells called mirror neurons. Your mirror neurons copy another person's behavior so that you share the same emotions. People with autism (see page 61) may have damage to their mirror neurons, making it harder for them to empathize with others.

Can I pretend to show emotions?

Most of us find it difficult to convincingly fake emotion. Actors, however, depend on the ability to display emotions that they do not actually feel. These actors are using body language, gestures, facial expressions, and eye contact to express the anger and fear that their characters are feeling. The most skilled actors are able to make an audience forget that the emotions are not real.

Making faces

Whether you are envious, confused, or happy, your facial expressions reveal your feelings to other people. These "windows" onto your emotions form a vital part of nonverbal communication. They are difficult to fake convincingly.

surprise

joy

disgust

fear

anger

sadness

Are facial expressions universal?

The "big six" facial expressions—surprise, joy, disgust, fear, anger, and sadness—are recognized worldwide and are "hard-wired" into your brain. Some other expressions mean different things in different parts of the world and are the result of culture rather than genes.

How do I make different faces?

Here you can see some of the 43 facial muscles that pull small areas of skin on your face. They work together to create thousands of different expressions. Two pairs of depressor muscles (4), for example, pull your lower lip and the corners of your mouth downward to express sadness.

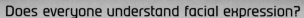

What makes me smile?

In the 1860s, French doctor Guillaume Duchenne investigated how we produce facial expressions. He applied electric probes to a patient's face so that specific muscles contracted. The resulting expressions were photographed.

Duchenne makes his patient smile.

How can I spot a fake smile?

This flight attendant's smile is fake. It is produced under conscious control and only uses muscles that pull the mouth sideways. Her eyes remain neutral and cold. A real smile is unconsciously triggered by your emotions and uses muscles that lift the lips and create wrinkles around "warm" eyes.

big grin but no warmth

1. The frontalis muscles raise the eyebrows and wrinkle the forehead.
2. Orbicularis oculi muscles close the eyelids.
3. Zygomaticus muscles pull the mouth up when you smile.
4. Depressor muscles pull the mouth down.

Does everyone understand facial expression?

Children with autism such as Megan (below) have problems relating to others. One reason for this is that these children find it difficult to recognize facial expressions. Here, Megan is interacting with Kaspar, a child-sized robot doll that can smile, frown, laugh, and gesture. Mimicking Kaspar will hopefully help Megan develop social interaction skills.

Megan copies Kaspar's gestures.

Fears and phobias

Fear is a natural, basic emotion that makes us alert to dangers. A phobia is different. It is an unnatural, persistent, and irrational fear of a specific thing—such as cats—or a situation—such as being high up—that disrupts a person's life.

What happens to my body when I'm scared?

Seeing, hearing, or just thinking about something scary—or that you have a phobia about—triggers the fight-or-flight reaction. Inside your brain, the amygdala (see page 58) generates a feeling of fear, anxiety, and even panic. It also sends a signal to the hypothalamus to prepare your body for attack or escape by increasing heart and breathing rates, energizing your leg muscles, and flooding your bloodstream with adrenaline, the "action hormone."

acrophobia—fear of heights
aerophobia—fear of flying
ailurophobia—fear of cats
aquaphobia—fear of water
arachnophobia—fear of spiders
astraphobia—fear of thunderstorms
bufonophobia—fear of toads
chiroptophobia—fear of bats
coulrophobia—fear of clowns
dendrophobia—fear of trees
gephyrophobia—fear of bridges
musophobia—fear of rats and mice
nephophobia—fear of clouds
nyctophobia—fear of darkness
ophidiophobia—fear of snakes
pediophobia—fear of dolls
pyrophobia—fear of fire
sciophobia—fear of shadows
selachophobia—fear of sharks
selenophobia—fear of the Moon
spheksophobia—fear of wasps

Can phobias be cured?

Most phobias are curable, especially if their cause—often a scary event in childhood—is known. There are several treatments, including drugs to reduce anxiety, psychotherapy to alter behavior, and desensitization (making the phobia sufferer less sensitive). Desensitization involves a person being gradually exposed to the object of their phobia—such as a spider—so that, over time, they feel less anxious about it.

Female or male?

What defines you as being female or male? Your sex is determined by two particular chromosomes of your 46 called sex chromosomes. Your gender—how you feel and show your femaleness or maleness—is influenced by genes and your upbringing and culture.

embryo
six weeks after
fertilization

Why are there two sexes?

Humans have two sexes because we evolved from animals that reproduce sexually. In sexual reproduction (see page 72), each sex has a precise role, with males producing sperm and females eggs. Sperm and eggs each carry 23 chromosomes and may carry different versions of genes. When a sperm and an egg meet at fertilization, the resulting offspring has a unique genetic makeup.

One of these
sperm will
fertilize the egg.

What determines my sex?

X and Y sex chromosomes decide your sex. Females have two X chromosomes (XX), while males have an X and a Y (XY). An egg always carries an X chromosome, while sperm (colored blue here) carry either X or Y. If a Y-carrying sperm fertilizes the egg, the embryo will start to develop male sex organs at six weeks and the baby will be a boy. If an X-carrying sperm fertilizes the egg, the baby will be a girl.

Females have XX chromosomes.

male XY sex chromosomes

female XX sex chromosomes

Is there a difference between sex and gender?

Sex refers to biological differences (see pages 72–73) between males and females. Gender is about the roles and activities that a society considers "appropriate" for males and females. Sex differences are not always clear-cut. Some people thought that 2009 world-champion woman athlete Caster Semenya was male, not female. They believed that she had an unfair advantage over the other athletes, so she had to prove that she is a woman.

Lea T

What is gender identity?

Gender identity describes whether we feel male or female. We express maleness or femaleness to others through our behavior—and it doesn't always match our biological sex. Brazilian supermodel Lea T (above) is biologically male, for example, but made her catwalk debut in 2011 as a woman.

Caster Semenya

TOYOTA

Semenya

berlin 2009

Brain differences

Do females and males behave in different ways? And, if so, is it because our brains differ, because of how we've been brought up . . . or a combination of both? Scientists have found that female and male brains are "wired" differently. But that doesn't alter the fact that either sex can take on any task—if we really want to!

dressing up:
a boy firefighter
and a girl fairy

Are brain differences present at birth?

Baby girls prefer to watch faces, while boys watch everything equally. As toddlers, most girls like to play with dolls, while many boys prefer toy cars. Gender differences seem to be present at birth but are later influenced by how a child is brought up.

Do I have a female or male brain?

Differences in female and male brains are due to the effects of hormones, such as testosterone (male hormone, see above right), before birth. Babies surrounded by more testosterone in the mother's womb are more likely to have a typically male brain. When performing complex tasks, the male brain is usually active on only one side, while the female brain uses both sides.

What is testosterone?

Testosterone is the male sex hormone. It makes an embryo male, triggers puberty, and maintains adult features such as a muscular, hairy body and deep voice. It also affects behavior, making males more competitive and—sometimes—more aggressive. Women produce testosterone, too. It helps maintain their bone mass.

Testosterone can make males more aggressive.

Are there typical male and female skills?

In theory, our brains give males and females distinct skills. Males are often good at technical matters, listing facts, and understanding maps. Females typically focus on writing and reading, empathy and feelings, and getting the bigger picture. But, in reality, most of us have a mix of male and female skills.

Like this welder, most of us have both male and female skills.

Forces of attraction

If people were not attracted to one another, reproduction would never happen and our species would die out. What do we find attractive in others? Perhaps it is their face . . . or even their smell!

Why are some faces more attractive than others?

Although body shape, intelligence, and personality all play a part in attraction, faces are very important. Both sexes are attracted to symmetrical faces, where the left side of the face exactly mirrors the right. For now, scientists can only guess at why we prefer symmetry. It may be that symmetry shows that a person has "good" genes to pass on.

What does "falling in love" mean?

This describes the feeling that two people have when they are very attracted to each other. Most people fall in love with someone of the opposite sex, but not all of us. When we fall in love, we experience a rush of excitement and pleasure caused by the release of a chemical in the brain. Love binds couples together, which helps if they are going to bring up children.

symmetrical
face

face with less
symmetry

Is there a love hormone?

Dubbed the "love hormone," oxytocin is made by the brain's hypothalamus and released into the bloodstream when people kiss and cuddle. Oxytocin gives people a pleasurable experience, makes them feel tenderness and affection, and strengthens the bond between them. When lovers are apart, a lack of oxytocin makes them pine for their partners.

crystals of the "love hormone" oxytocin

Are body smells attractive?

Smell does seem to play a part in attraction. Certain body odors are linked to substances called MHC proteins, which vary from person to person. People may be subconsciously attracted to partners who have different MHC proteins to their own. The reason? It's been suggested that parents with dissimilar MHC proteins produce a healthier child. Their child inherits a greater range of MHC proteins, which play a vital role in fighting disease.

Tennis star Rafael Nadal shakes sweat, which carries body odors, from his hair.

Does cosmetic surgery improve on nature?

How you look is part of your identity, but some people feel insecure about their attractiveness. More and more women and men are turning to cosmetic surgery, such as face-lifts, lip plumping, or nose resculpting. While some people have surgery to reverse the effects of aging, others do it to improve their attractiveness, perhaps by making their faces more symmetrical. Cosmetic surgery can, however, have the opposite effect by distorting or unbalancing facial features.

face after repeated cosmetic surgery

Brain trainers

See how well your amazing
brain absorbed the facts in Chapter 3.

1. The six basic facial expressions are joy,
surprise, disgust, fear, anger, and . . . what else?

2. Unscramble BEST SLY MIMIC to get the part
of your brain that deals with emotions.

3. Chiroptophobia is an irrational fear of:
a) bats
b) helicopters
c) feet

Answers on
page 90.

Hello!

Did you recognize the
languages used for the
greetings on pages 52–53?

Bonjour!—French; **Ciao!**—Italian
Guten Tag!—German; **Hello!**—English
¡Hola!—Spanish; **Konnichiwa!**—Japanese
Namaste!—Hindi; **Ni hao!**—Chinese
Shalom!—Hebrew; **Witaj!**—Polish

Where to look?

Your brain expects a face to be defined
by two eyes, one nose, and a mouth.
A picture like this confuses its
face-recognition area and makes
viewing uncomfortable.

Conscientious or disorganized?

This personality quiz is
continued from page 50.

3. When it comes to my bedroom:
a) I always make sure that it's
neat and clean
b) I try to keep it clean but often
need to be reminded
c) I like living in a complete mess

Continued on page 90.

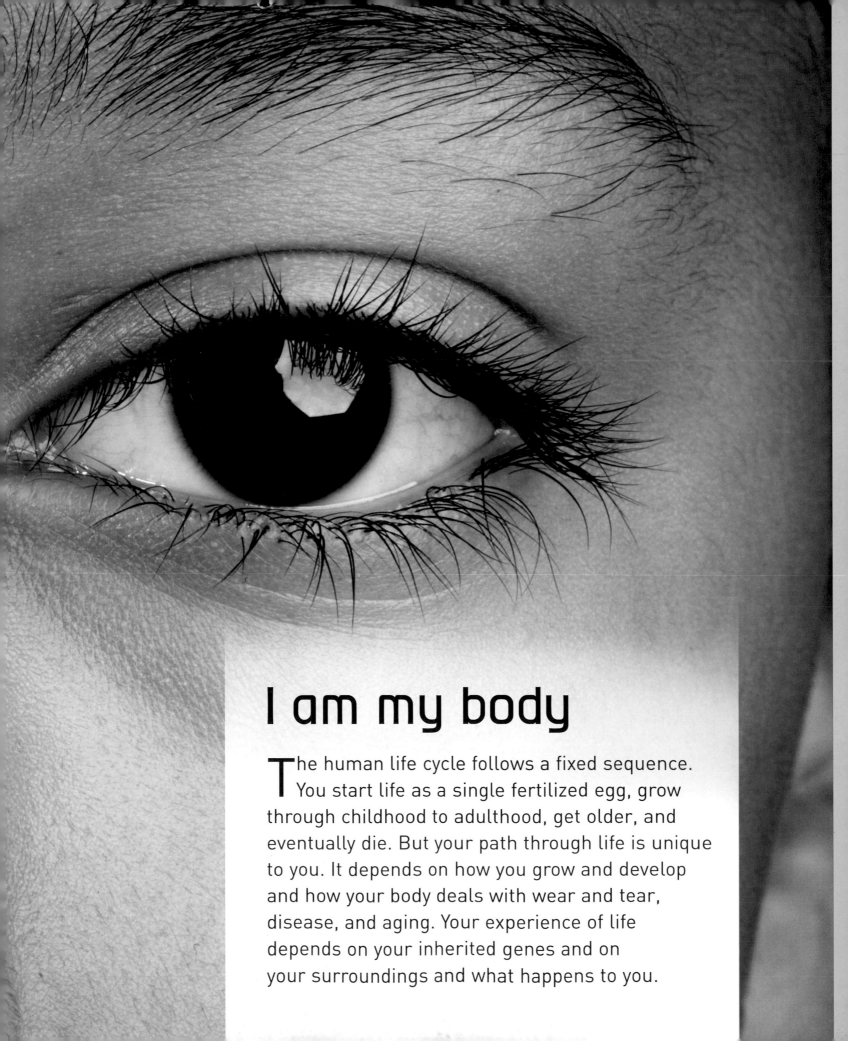

I am my body

The human life cycle follows a fixed sequence. You start life as a single fertilized egg, grow through childhood to adulthood, get older, and eventually die. But your path through life is unique to you. It depends on how you grow and develop and how your body deals with wear and tear, disease, and aging. Your experience of life depends on your inherited genes and on your surroundings and what happens to you.

Making me

Humans use a process called sexual reproduction to have children. The male and female reproductive systems consist of specialized sex organs that produce sex cells called, respectively, sperm and eggs. These cells join together at fertilization to produce a baby that differs genetically from both of its parents.

egg

sperm

1. The testes make millions of sperm daily.
2. The vas deferens carries sperm to the penis.
3. The penis introduces sperm into the woman's vagina.

Which are the reproductive organs?

Male and female reproductive organs are different. During an intimate act called sexual intercourse, sperm made in a man's testes pass from his penis into the woman's vagina. Fertilization happens in a fallopian tube if a sperm meets an egg within 24 hours of its release from an ovary.

A hydra bud splits from its parent.

The male reproductive system produces sperm.

Do all living things reproduce using sexual reproduction?

No. Some simpler organisms use asexual reproduction, which needs only one parent and can quickly produce many offspring. The parent divides or, like this hydra, buds to produce new organisms that are genetically identical. The disadvantage is that, because all of the offspring are the same, none has a better chance of surviving disease, predators, or a change in conditions.

4. Mammary glands in the breasts produce milk after birth.

5. The ovaries produce eggs and usually release one each month.

6. A fallopian tube receives an egg from an ovary and carries it to the uterus; the tube is the site of fertilization if it occurs.

7. The uterus protects and nourishes the fetus during pregnancy.

8. The vagina is the passage through which the baby is born.

The female reproductive system releases eggs and nourishes the fertilized egg as it develops.

What is IVF?

In vitro fertilization (IVF), which takes place outside the body, may help women who cannot become pregnant. Doctors take eggs from a woman's ovaries and sperm from her partner. They fertilize the eggs with the sperm in a laboratory. The resulting tiny embryo is put into her uterus to develop into a baby.

Sperm may be injected into an egg during IVF.

What's special about sex cells?

Most body cells reproduce using mitosis. One cell splits into two offspring cells, each with identical copies of the parent cell's two sets of chromosomes (see page 34). But cells that produce sperm and eggs are different because they use a type of cell division called meiosis. This creates sex cells with only one set of chromosomes. At fertilization, the sperm and egg fuse to restore the normal two sets.

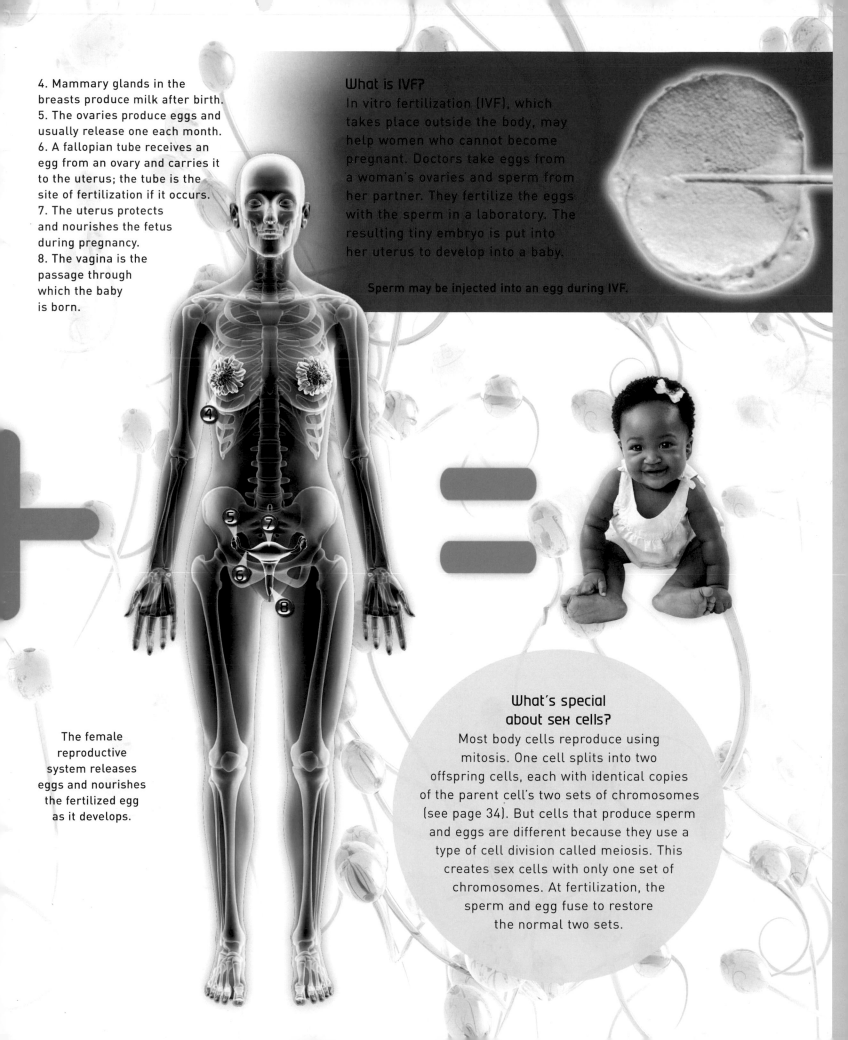

New developments

You started life as a single cell: a fertilized egg. How did this egg, eventually, develop into a person consisting of 100 trillion cells? Genes control most of this process of cell division and growth. They make sure that all of the right parts grow in the right places.

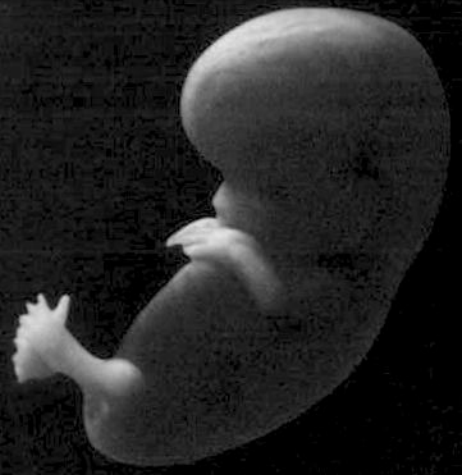

embryo at
7 weeks

How did I grow from a ball of cells?

At the start of pregnancy, the fertilized egg divides repeatedly. It implants into the lining of the mother's uterus (womb) and forms an embryo with a head, body, limbs, and organs, such as the heart and brain. Eight weeks after fertilization, you became a fetus. About thirty-two weeks later, you had developed as much as you could in the womb. You were ready to be born.

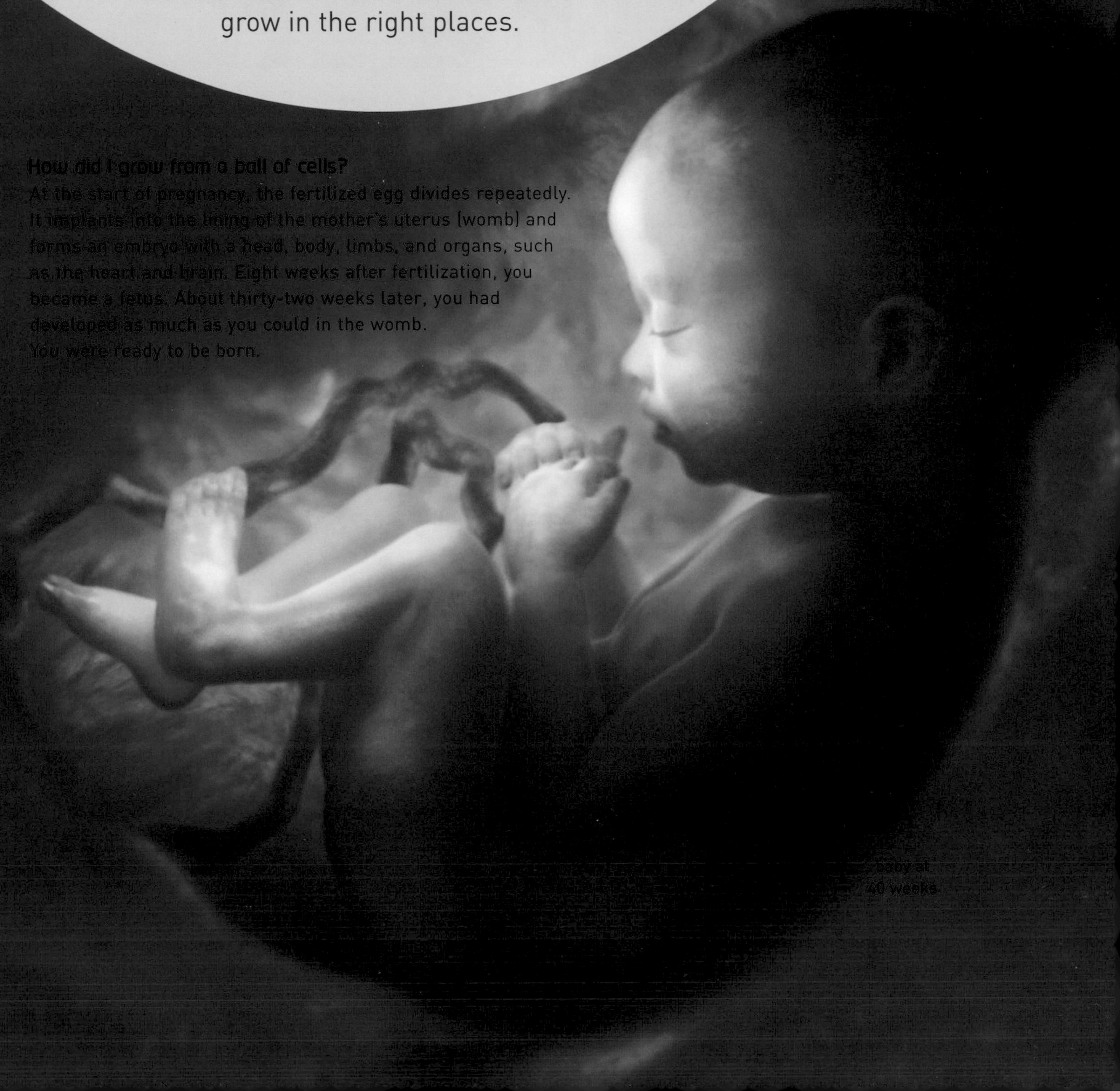

baby at
40 weeks

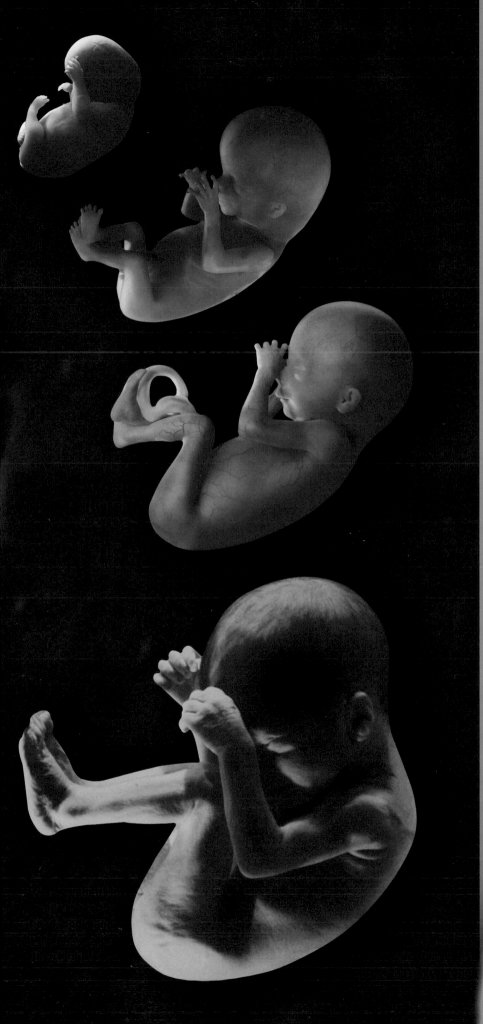

How do doctors check on a developing baby?

Ultrasound scanning is used to "see" a developing fetus as it grows inside its mother's uterus. A technician sends harmless high-frequency sound waves into the mother's abdomen. These waves bounce off the fetus and are analyzed by a computer to produce an image that is viewed on a screen. Ultrasound scanning is used to check the baby's heartbeat and health. It can also be used to tell whether the mother is expecting a baby boy or girl.

scanning a baby using ultrasound

If all body cells have identical genes, why do they look different?

At first, an embryo is made up of identical unspecialized cells called embryonic stem cells. As the embryo develops, different genes turn on or off inside the stem cells. The genes create the precise instructions to turn the stem cells into specific types of cells, such as nerve or muscle cells. In the future, stem cells may be used to repair or replace our damaged cells, tissues, or even organs (see page 89).

Claiming my inheritance

Genetics is the study of inheritance—how genes are passed on from one generation to the next or sometimes skip a generation. You inherit a selection of genes from your parents, and this gives you your own unique genetic makeup.

How do genes affect the way I look?

Your genes control how your cells work, and they, in turn, affect the way you look. Most of your outside features, from the shape of your ears to the relative sizes of your toes, are the result of several genes working together. Having a tongue you can roll is genetic, too—though it is possible to learn how to tongue roll with practice!

widow's peak (hairline shape)

convex nose

hitchhiker's thumb (curves backward)

Are all of my genes as powerful as the rest?

You inherit two sets of genes, one from each parent. Within these two sets, you may have different alleles (versions) of particular genes (see page 35). Some alleles are recessive; some are dominant. Recessive alleles have an effect only if two are present. If a dominant allele is present, it will overpower the effect of the recessive allele.

This peacock has inherited two recessive alleles that make its feathers white.

freely hanging (rather than attached) earlobe

tongue rolling

cleft chin

a *Lebensborn* family

What was eugenics?

Eugenics was the terrible and now discredited belief that, since all of our characteristics are inherited, only people with "superior" genes should be allowed to breed. Eugenics was taken to horrifying extremes in the 1930s and 1940s in Nazi Germany. The Nazi *Lebensborn* programme encouraged "racially pure" Germans to breed, while the mentally and physically disabled were murdered.

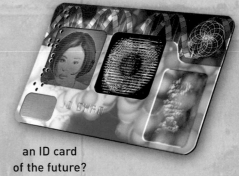

an ID card of the future?

Do we know what all genes do?

The Human Genome Project (see page 38) identified that we have around 23,000 genes. But we're still a long way from knowing what all of our genes do—not to mention the different alleles (versions) of genes. One day, we may carry details of our genetic makeup on an ID card. This information could be used for good or bad, however. Not everyone welcomes a future where we're all known inside out.

Nature and nurture

The way we—and other animals—look and behave doesn't just depend on our genes (nature). Our environment (nurture) has an effect, too. Together, nature and nurture interact to give us our unique features.

Clown fish are reef-living, warm-water fish.

Famine may alter our genes.

What decides my body size?

The genes you inherit from your parents are a big influence on whether you are tall or short, muscular or skinny. But your body size and shape also depend on environment and lifestyle—for example, how healthy your diet is and how much you exercise. Some lifestyle factors may directly affect genes. Suffering from starvation can cause harmful changes to genes that might be passed on. During the Dutch Hunger Winter (1944–1945), people starved. Children conceived during that time (conception is when an egg is fertilized) went on to have higher rates of health problems.

sumo wrestlers

Are sumo wrestlers born overweight? Japanese sumo wrestlers rely on bulk to force opponents out of the ring—but they aren't born bulky. They eat good amounts of rice, noodles, and chanko (a protein-rich stew). This diet, along with plenty of sleep, makes them pile on extra weight. But how quickly a wrestler gains weight also depends on his or her genes.

Are queen honeybees the same as workers?

Within a honeybee colony, a queen and her female workers share the same genes. Yet she is bigger, lives for years, and lays eggs, while they live for only a few weeks and are infertile. The difference is that, as a developing grub, the queen is fed with protein-rich royal jelly. This interacts with her genes, turning some on or off to make her a queen.

queen honeybee (center) with workers

Is sex always controlled by genes?

In most animals, only genes determine sex, but sometimes, outside influences play a part. Clown fish groups consist of a breeding female and male and several nonbreeding males. When the female dies, the breeding male switches its sex to become female, and the biggest nonbreeder becomes the breeding male. Environment affects sex in other animals, too. Whether alligator hatchlings are male or female depends on the temperature in the nest where they develop.

Can environment affect an animal's color?

Yes! Like other cats, a Siamese has a gene that controls the manufacture of the dark pigment (coloring) melanin. But a gene mutation in the Siamese means that melanin production is affected by its body temperature—in other words, the environment. Melanin production works normally in the cat's cooler extremities, such as the ears and nose, which are dark colored, but not in warmer body parts, such as its chest, back, and belly, which remain white.

A Siamese cat has a dark nose and ears.

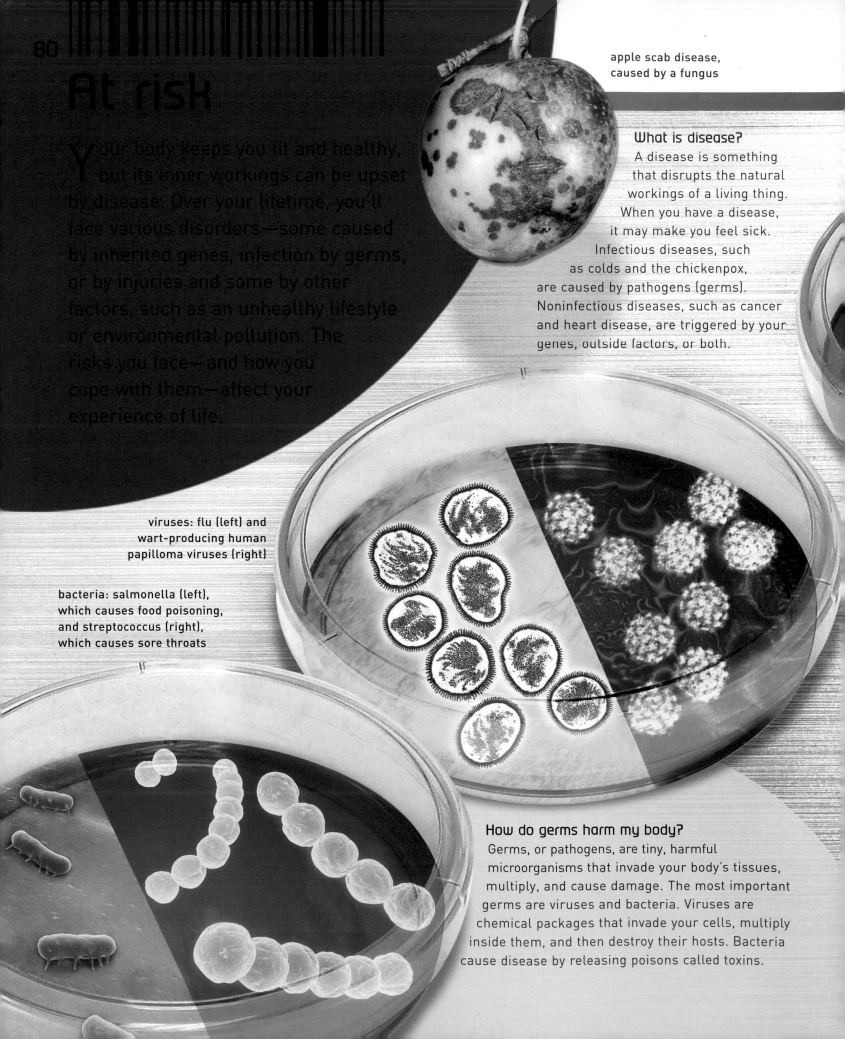

At risk

Your body keeps you fit and healthy, but its inner workings can be upset by disease. Over your lifetime, you'll face various disorders—some caused by inherited genes, infection by germs, or by injuries and some by other factors, such as an unhealthy lifestyle or environmental pollution. The risks you face—and how you cope with them—affect your experience of life.

apple scab disease, caused by a fungus

What is disease?

A disease is something that disrupts the natural workings of a living thing. When you have a disease, it may make you feel sick. Infectious diseases, such as colds and the chickenpox, are caused by pathogens (germs). Noninfectious diseases, such as cancer and heart disease, are triggered by your genes, outside factors, or both.

viruses: flu (left) and wart-producing human papilloma viruses (right)

bacteria: salmonella (left), which causes food poisoning, and streptococcus (right), which causes sore throats

How do germs harm my body?

Germs, or pathogens, are tiny, harmful microorganisms that invade your body's tissues, multiply, and cause damage. The most important germs are viruses and bacteria. Viruses are chemical packages that invade your cells, multiply inside them, and then destroy their hosts. Bacteria cause disease by releasing poisons called toxins.

What is cancer?

Cancer is the name for a group of diseases, all caused by changes in a cell's DNA. The resulting abnormal cell multiplies out of control and produces a tumor—a growth that affects the surrounding tissues. Untreated, cancer cells spread around the body and create more tumors, often resulting in death. People can reduce their risk of developing some cancers—for example, by avoiding cigarettes (lung cancer) or overexposure to sunlight (skin cancer). Some people inherit genes that put them at a greater risk of certain cancers, such as breast, ovarian, and bowel cancers.

cancer cells dividing

Can you inherit a disease?

More than 10,000 diseases called genetic disorders are caused by inheriting disease-causing genes from one or both parents. People with sickle cell anemia, for example, inherit a gene that produces abnormal hemoglobin, the protein that fills red blood cells and carries oxygen. Red blood cells containing abnormal hemoglobin are sickle shaped, block blood flow, cause pain, and carry less oxygen, resulting in breathlessness.

normal (round) and sickle or crescent shaped red blood cells

Defenses and treatments

Day and night, invading pathogens threaten your well-being. Your immune system fights off most of these attacks. Modern medicine provides extra help in the form of vaccines and drugs. Exactly how much help you need depends on you, the individual.

killer T cells (pink)
attacking a cancer cell

What's special about my immune system?

Your immune system is a unique record of the diseases you've fought and beaten. It includes defensive white blood cells, such as T and B lymphocytes, in your blood and lymphatic systems. T cells attack pathogens and "rogue" cancer cells, while B cells release antibodies that disable germs. Both remember and adapt to pathogens so that they can better fight them in the future.

How does HIV disable the immune system?

Helper T cells make sure that our other lymphocytes (immune system cells) work properly. But they can be infected and destroyed by HIV viruses that multiply inside them. The number of helper T cells plummets, weakening the immune system and leading to the development of AIDS.

a helper T cell
infected by HIV (red)

the lymphatic system

Why do I have to be vaccinated?

Some pathogens can overwhelm your body before your immune system has time to respond. Vaccination introduces a harmless version of a pathogen—for example, the polio virus—into your body. Your T and B lymphocytes react to and remember the harmless pathogen so that your immune system is primed to destroy the "real" version if it ever invades.

a child being given an oral polio vaccine

Do drugs work the same way in everyone?

We don't all react in the same way to drugs prescribed to treat illness. Depending on the person, a particular drug might have no effect, work normally, or have side effects. This is because of tiny differences in our genes. Individual genetic analysis means that doctors are already beginning to give us customized drugs, tailored to our individual genetic makeup.

How does gene therapy work?

Some diseases are caused because we have a particular version of a gene. Gene therapy involves putting a "correct" version of the gene into the affected cells so that they work normally. One possible method is using stem cells that carry a normal gene, because stem cells can give rise to any tissue type (see page 75). Inside the body, the stem cells can produce tissue cells that work properly.

storing stem cells

Getting older

Aging is a natural part of the human life cycle—inevitable and unavoidable. It also forms part of your identity. As you get older, your body will gradually wear out as its cells become less able to repair damage to themselves and their DNA. How rapidly this occurs depends on your genes, but it is also affected by your lifestyle. Staying healthy and active can help you live a longer, better life.

What are the main signs of aging?

As you get older, your skin gets less elastic, wrinkles appear, and your hair turns gray or white or falls out. Your hearing and vision may become less efficient. Some people develop dementia, a condition that makes them forget things and that can affect their personality. Other signs of old age include weakening muscles and problems with the joints.

Exercise reduces stress.

Can I slow down the aging process?

Yes. Regular exercise strengthens your muscles and bones and, with a balanced diet, helps you maintain a healthy weight. You can limit wrinkles by staying out of the sun and not smoking cigarettes. It's also sensible to avoid stress and keep your brain active.

Will my identity change as I get older?

Aging affects your appearance and the way people see you, so that aspect of your identity will change. And as time goes on, you will go through more experiences—both good and bad—and these will shape your personality. Yet many older people say that they feel the same as they did when they were younger. Some take advantage of the extra time they have when they stop working to travel or try out new things, such as skydiving!

skydiving

Why are older people's bones more likely to break?

Throughout life, our bones are constantly rebuilt. But as we age, our body becomes less able to renew bone tissue. At the same time, our bones become less dense and more likely to break. This problem particularly affects people, mostly women, who suffer from osteoporosis.

thinning of bone tissue as a result of osteoporosis

Living forever

Some animals and plants live for many hundreds of years. The human life span is much shorter. However, thanks to better diets and health care, people in developed countries are living longer than previous generations. But could humans ever live forever?

Jeanne Calment lived for 122 years and 164 days.

Why can't I live forever?

One of the reasons is that, over time, your cells wear out and cannot be repaired. During cell division, telomeres (shown in red here) protect the ends of chromosomes from damage. As you age, telomeres shorten—chromosomes "fray" and lose DNA instructions. Eventually, cells stop dividing. Then they (and you) die.

Could I live for a thousand years?

When Jeanne Calment of Arles, France, died in 1997, she set a record for human life span. Could you break her record and live longer—perhaps for as long as a thousand years? It's unlikely with existing technology because of the limit that your genes and lifestyle impose on your life span.

scarlet macaw, 80 years

giant tortoise, 150 years

red sea urchin, 200 years

bowhead whale, 200 years

Which are the oldest living things on Earth?

South America's scarlet macaw has a similar life span to that of humans but is easily outlived by the other species in this gallery. The quahog, a North American cold-water clam, lives for around 400 years. And all are beaten by the world's oldest organism, the slow-growing Californian Jurupa oak, thought to be 13,000 years old.

Could eating less help me live longer?

Research shows that mice fed on a strict diet live longer. Could the same be true for humans? Scientists believe that eating less would not have such dramatic effects for you. However, exercising and avoiding junk foods, such as burgers and fries, should improve your health.

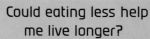

Ushi Okushima, an Okinawan woman, aged 109 (in 2011)

Where do people live the longest?

Okinawa, Japan, is a hot spot for centenarians (people aged over 100). Its residents live the longest, healthiest lives. Studies suggest that both genes and diet contribute to their longevity. Okinawans have versions of genes that enable their cells to repair damage more efficiently.

Repairs and replacements

Some animals have the power to rebuild body parts, but humans don't. If you lose organs or limbs through damage or disease, you cannot regenerate them. Fortunately, modern medicine is finding ways to repair the body, using replacement body parts.

Might scientists be able to grow complex organs in a lab one day?

Can we grow new organs?

Scientists have already grown some organs, including skin and the trachea (windpipe). They use stem cells from the patient so that his or her body recognizes the replacement organ as its own and doesn't attack it. Someday, scientists may be able to grow very complex organs, such as the heart or lungs.

What are bionic limbs?

Bionic limbs are lifelike artificial arms and legs that move owing to electric motors. The latest ones can be controlled by brainpower! When Claudia Mitchell (left) of Arkansas lost her arm in a car accident in 2006, she became the first woman to be fitted with a thought-controlled bionic limb. When Claudia thinks about using the arm, a computer inside the arm detects the electrical signals from her brain and instructs electric motors to make the movement happen.

Which animals can grow new body parts?

No bird or mammal can, but many other animals, from starfish and lobsters to salamanders and lizards, regrow body parts. If threatened by a hungry predator, for example, a gecko may shed its tail. The fallen-off tail wiggles, distracting the predator while the lizard gets away. Over the coming months, the gecko slowly regrows a replacement tail.

a gecko growing a new tail

pigs carrying human genes

What is a transplant?

A transplant occurs when a replacement organ, such as a kidney or the liver, is taken from one person (the donor) and put in the body of someone else (the recipient). The recipient takes medicine that stops his or her immune system from trying to destroy the "alien" organ. There are never enough donor organs. Scientists have even bred animals with human genes in the hope of harvesting their organs, but now they're investigating other solutions. One possibility is growing replacement organs (see above left).

Brain trainers

See how well your amazing
brain absorbed the facts in Chapter 4.

1. Unscramble IT LAZIER IF NOT to find
what happens when a sperm and egg meet.

2. In which country is there a "hot spot" for
centenarians (people aged 100 or more)?

3. Bacteria and other tiny organisms that
cause disease are called:
a) pathfinders
b) pathogens
c) pathologists

Answers
below right.

Did you know?

• The science of genetics
was founded by an Austrian
monk named Gregor Mendel. He
studied inheritance in pea plants and
published his results in 1866—but his
work was ignored for the next 35 years.

• All of the eggs that a girl will ever
produce—hundreds of thousands
of them—are already present
when she is born.

Digital age

Want to know what you
might look like when you get
older? Type "face-aging software" into an
Internet search engine and see what comes up.

Conscientious or disorganized?

This personality quiz is
continued from page 70.

4. As far as homework is concerned:
a) I always hand it in on time
b) I usually hand it in on time but
have been late
c) it's usually late, but I'm good at
making up excuses

Find out what you're like in
the panel on the right.

Am I? . . .

How did you do in the
personality quizzes?
Score 10 for each a),
5 for each b), and 0 for
each c).

page 10:
Extrovert or introvert?
How many points did
you score?
30–40: you are more
likely to be an extrovert
10–30: you're a
little of both
0–10: you're more likely
to be an introvert

pages 30, 50, 70, and 90:
Conscientious or disorganized?
How many points did
you score?
30–40: you are more
likely to be
conscientious
10–30: you're a
little of both
0–10: you're more likely
to be disorganized

Brain trainers
page 30
1. False. It's 100 billion;
2. phrenology; 3. c) IQ
(intelligence quotient)
page 50
1. Francis Crick and
James Watson, helped
by Rosalind Franklin;
2. c) Africa;
3. chromosomes
page 70
1. sadness; 2. limbic
system; 3. a) bats
page 90
1. fertilization; 2. Japan
(the hot spot is
Okinawa);
3. b) pathogens

Glossary

adrenaline A fast-acting hormone released by the adrenal gland that prepares the body for rapid action at times of threat or danger.

AIDS (acquired immune deficiency syndrome) A disease that occurs when HIV has damaged the body's immune system so much that it can no longer fight off other infections and diseases.

allele One of two or more alternative versions of the same gene.

amino acid One of 20 chemical substances that are the building blocks of proteins.

amygdala An almond-shaped structure in the brain's limbic system that plays a key role in emotions.

ancestor A person who lived a long, long time ago, from whom others are descended.

antibody A substance released by immune system cells that disables pathogens, such as bacteria, and marks them for destruction.

archaeologist A person who studies human history and prehistory by excavating ancient sites and examining artifacts, skeletons, and other remains.

asexual reproduction A type of reproduction that involves only one parent and that produces offspring that are genetically identical to that parent.

autism A range of disorders that make it difficult to form relationships and communicate with others.

bacteria (singular: bacterium) A group of simple single-celled organisms, some of which cause diseases in humans.

base One of four chemical substances—adenine (A), thymine (T), cytosine (C), and guanine (G)—that spell out the coded instructions in DNA. A, C, and G occur in RNA, but thymine is replaced by uracil (U).

biological sex The state of being male or female depending on the 23rd pair of chromosomes—two Xs make a person female; an X and a Y make him male.

bionic Describes an artificial replacement body part that is usually operated electrically.

brain The body's control center, made up of soft nervous tissue and contained inside the skull. Its largest part is the cerebrum. Other parts include the cerebellum, which coordinates movement and balance, and the brain stem, which controls breathing and heart rate.

CAT (computerized axial tomography) A scanning technique that produces images of living tissues using x-rays and a computer.

cell The tiny living unit from which all organisms, including humans, are made.

cell division The process by which cells multiply by splitting in half.

central nervous system (CNS) The brain and spinal cord.

cerebral cortex The thin outer layer of the cerebrum that processes information relating to the senses, movement, thought, and memory.

cerebrum The largest part of the brain, which is divided into two halves, or hemispheres.

chemical A substance that has its own unique structure and properties.

chromosome In humans, one of 46 threadlike structures, composed of DNA and proteins, that are found inside the nucleus of most cells.

codon A sequence of three base letters of genetic code that together represents a specific amino acid.

dementia A loss of brain function that is most commonly found in older people. Signs of dementia include memory loss, personality change, and poor reasoning.

DNA (deoxyribonucleic acid) A substance found in the nucleus of a cell, made up of spiral molecules that carry genes.

DNA profiling Also known as DNA fingerprinting, the technique used to identify a person by the unique features in his or her DNA.

dominant Describes an allele that "overpowers" another allele of the same gene to produce a particular feature in an organism. The "overpowered" allele is known as recessive.

egg A female sex cell; also called an ovum.

embryo The name given to a developing baby during the first eight weeks after fertilization.

embryonic stem cell A cell that has the ability to develop into all types of body cells.

emotion A strong feeling, such as joy, fear, anger, sadness, surprise, or disgust.

empathy The ability to understand another person's feelings.

energy The capacity to perform work. Cells need energy to function and stay alive.

environment The surroundings, including the family, in which a person grows up and lives.

enzyme A type of protein that speeds up the rate of chemical reactions inside and outside cells, thereby making life possible.

eugenics The study of ways of "improving" the human population through controlled breeding, popular in the 1900s but now regarded as wrong and immoral.

evolution The process by which living organisms change gradually over very long periods of time and that gives rise to new species.

fertilization The joining together of an egg and a sperm to produce a new living organism.

fetus The name given to a developing baby from the ninth week after fertilization until birth.

fMRI (functional magnetic resonance imaging) A type of MRI that analyzes blood flow to produce images of brain activity.

forensic Describes the use of scientific methods—such as analyzing fingerprints or bloodstains—to solve crimes.

fungi (singular: fungus) A group of organisms, including yeasts, molds, and mushrooms, that are neither animals nor plants. Some fungi cause diseases.

gender The state of being female or male. It usually matches biological sex, but not always—it is determined by the sorts of behaviors and roles that a person adopts.

gene One of the 23,000 instructions, each one a section of a DNA molecule within a chromosome, that are needed to build and run the human body.

genome The DNA contained in one set of chromosomes.

hard-wired Describes a behavior that is built into the brain at birth, not learned.

hippocampus A part of the brain's limbic system that plays key roles in storing long-term memories and in spatial awareness.

HIV (human immunodeficiency virus) A virus that infects and destroys immune system cells, weakens the body's defenses, and leads to AIDS.

Homo sapiens The species to which humans belong.

hormone A substance released into the blood by an endocrine gland that changes the activities of target cells and tissues.

Hox genes A set of genes that control the basic structure of most animals, from fruit flies to humans.

Human Genome Project (HGP) A research program, carried out between 1990 and 2003, to discover the sequence of bases in human DNA and identify all of the genes in the human genome.

hypothalamus A small but important part of the brain that controls many body activities and that links the nervous and endocrine (hormonal) systems.

immune system The body's major defense mechanism. It consists mostly of white blood cells in the circulatory and lymphatic systems, which destroy invading pathogens.

inherit To receive from one's parents or ancestors.

larynx Also called the voice box, the structure at the top of the trachea (windpipe) that contains the vocal cords and produces sounds.

limbic system A collection of structures within the brain that play important roles in emotions and memory.

longevity Long life.

lymphatic system A network of vessels that drain excess fluid from the tissues and house white blood cells.

maternal chromosomes A set of 23 chromosomes in a person's cells inherited from his or her mother.

meiosis A type of cell division that happens in the testes and ovaries and that produces sex cells—sperm and eggs—that carry one set of chromosomes.

melanin A dark pigment that colors the skin, hair, and the iris of the eye.

microscopic Describes something so small that it can be seen only through a microscope.

mitochondria Tiny structures inside a cell that release energy, enabling the cell to perform all of its tasks.

mitosis The type of cell division involved in growth and repair that produces two cells identical to the "parent" cell.

molecule A chemical unit made up of two or more atoms.

MRI (magnetic resonance imaging) A scanning technique that produces images of living tissues using magnetism, radio waves, and a computer.

mRNA (messenger RNA) A type of RNA that copies the coded instructions in a section of DNA and carries them to a ribosome, where proteins can be made.

mtDNA (mitochondrial DNA) A circular DNA molecule found only inside the mitochondria, or energy-releasing structures, of cells.

mutation A change in the base sequence of DNA caused by an error in copying or some other factor that may be passed on to offspring.

natural selection The "weeding-out" process that is the driving force of evolution, favoring organisms that are best suited to their surroundings and therefore more likely to survive and pass on their favorable genes.

nerve A bundle of neurons that relays nerve impulses between the body and central nervous system.

nerve impulse An electrical signal that is transmitted along a neuron at high speed.

neuron One of the interconnected nerve cells that make up the nervous system.

noncoding DNA The sections of an organism's DNA that do not contain instructions for making proteins.

nucleus The control center of a cell, which contains chromosomes. It is surrounded by the nuclear membrane.

organ A body part, such as the heart and brain, that is made of two or more types of tissues and that has a specific function or functions.

organism Any single living thing, from a bacterium to a human being.

osteoporosis A disease that makes bones brittle and fragile.

oxytocin A hormone—sometimes called the "love hormone"—that plays a part in human attraction, as well as in birth.

paternal chromosomes A set of 23 chromosomes in a person's cells inherited from his or her father.

pathogen A microorganism, such as a bacterium, that causes disease in humans.

PET (positron emission tomography) A scanning technique that produces images of brain activity by detecting radiation emitted by substances injected into the body.

polio A disease caused by a virus that can cause permanent paralysis in some people.

prehistoric From the time in human history before written records began.

protein One of a group of substances that perform many roles inside the body, including as enzymes and antibodies, and that are constructed using instructions contained in genes.

recessive Describes an allele that is overpowered by another allele of the same gene and, as a result, does not produce a particular feature in an organism. The allele that overpowers it is known as dominant.

REM (rapid eye movement) sleep A stage of light sleep during which the brain is very active and dreaming occurs.

ribosome A tiny structure inside a cell, on which proteins are made.

RNA (ribonucleic acid) A substance made within living cells that copies and translates the instructions stored in DNA to make proteins.

sex chromosome One of two chromosomes inside each body cell that determine a person's sex.

sexual intercourse An intimate act between two adults during which a man's penis is introduced into a woman's vagina so that sperm can be released there.

sexual reproduction A type of reproduction that involves male and female parents that produce sex cells that then fuse to produce offspring.

species A group of similar organisms, such as modern humans (Homo sapiens), that can breed together and produce offspring.

sperm A male sex cell.

STR (short tandem repeat) A pattern of repeat sequences of bases in a person's DNA that is used in DNA profiling.

system A group of linked organs, such as those in the digestive system, that work together to do a specific task or tasks.

telomere A region at the end of a chromosome that protects it from damage during cell division.

testosterone A male sex hormone that triggers the development of, and maintains, male sexual features.

tissue A group of the same or similar types of cells that cooperate to carry out a particular task.

toxin A poison that is released into body tissues.

transplant The replacement of a diseased organ with a healthy living organ from a donor.

tRNA (transfer RNA) A type of RNA that plays a key part in translating the instructions carried by mRNA to build a protein.

vaccine A medication that contains a weakened form of a pathogen and that is introduced into the body to boost our defenses against the "real" form.

virus A nonliving infectious agent that causes diseases, such as the flu, when it invades body cells to reproduce.

vocal cords Two membranes that are stretched across the larynx and that vibrate to produce sounds.

X chromosome One of two types of sex chromosomes, the presence of a pair of which determines a person is female.

Y chromosome One of two types of sex chromosomes, the presence of which determines that a person is male.

Index

Acknowledgments

The publisher would like to thank the following for permission to reproduce their material. Every care has been taken to trace copyright holders. However, if there have been unintentional omissions or failure to trace copyright holders, we apologize and will, if informed, endeavor to make corrections in any future edition. b = bottom, c = center, l = left, t = top, m = middle

cover (crowd) Getty/Image Bank; (brain scan) Shutterstock/Fedor Kondratenko; (eye test) Science Photo Library (SPL)/David Nicholls; (mitosis) SPL/Dr. Richard Kessel & Dr. Gene Shih/Visuals Unlimited; (blood) Shutterstock/Zoltan Pataki; (snowboarder) Shutterstock/Ipatov; (scientist) SPL/BSIP/PIKO; (fish) Shutterstock; (chimp) Alamy/Juniors Bildarchiv; (man) Shutterstock/Suzanne Tucker; (mom) Shutterstock/Artpose Adam Borkowski; (girl) Shutterstock/Tish1; (DNA) SPL/Mehau Kulyk; (babies) Corbis/Comet; (sperm) SPL/Susumu Nishinaga; (neurons) Shutterstock/ Sebastian Kaulitzki; (virus) Shutterstock/Jezper; title page SPL/Alex Bartel; page 2tl Shutterstock/SARANS; 2tr Shutterstock/Blacqbook; 2ctl Shutterstock/alison1414; 2cr Shutterstock/Sebastian Kaulitzki; 2cbl Shutterstock/Viktoriya; 2bl Shutterstock/lanynch; 2br Shutterstock; 3tc Shutterstock/dream designs; 3tr Shutterstock/Ipatov; 3c Shutterstock/Dmitriy Shironosov; 3cr Shutterstock/Daniel Koreniewski; 4cl Shutterstock/Galushko Sergey; 4tr Shutterstock/James Thew; 4cr Shutterstock/Sebastian Kaulitzki; 5tr Shutterstock/Vivid Pixels; 5bl Shutterstock/Tishenko Irina; 6t Shutterstock/Imagesbycat; 6cr Corbis/Gideon Mendel; 7t Corbis/BSPI; 7c Corbis/Floris Leeuvenberg; 7bl NASA; 7br Corbis/moodboard; 8t Corbis/George Shelley; 8b Corbis/Tim Pannell; 9tr Getty/Photodisc; 9cl Corbis/Steven Vidler; 9br Corbis/Gunter Marx; 11 SPL/Geoff Tompkinson; 12 Shutterstock/Sebastian Kaulitzki; 12c Shutterstock/Sebastian Kaulitzki; 12r SPL/Steve Gschmeissner; 13br Frank Lane Picture Agency/Suzi Esterhas/Minden; 14 SPL/Nancy Kedersha; 14b Shutterstock; 14c SPL/GJLP; 14cr SPL/Patrick Lanmann; 15tl Shutterstock/mamahoohooba; 15c Shutterstock/Donald P. Oehman; 15c (brain) Corbis/John W. Karapelou, CMI; 15br SPL/Philippe Psaila; 16 Getty/Photodisc; 16l Alamy/Mark Sykes; 17tl SPL/M-edical Images, Universal Images Group; 17tl (fig leaf) Shutterstock/sarah2; 17cl Prof. Jeff Lichtman, Harvard Medical School; 17cr SPL/Sovereign, ISM; 17b Shutterstock/RoxyFer; 18 Shutterstock/jeka84; 18t Shutterstock/YanLev; 18b Shutterstock/Suzanne Tucker; 19tl Shutterstock/Ipatov; 19tr Shutterstock/Piligrim; 19c Alamy/Big Cheese Photo LLC; 19bl Alamy/Image Source; 19bcl Alamy/LA Heusinkeld; 19bcr Shutterstock/photomarket; 19br Shutterstock/mexrix; 19b Shutterstock/MedusArt; 20 Shutterstock/Brandon Seidel; 20cr Shutterstock/cybrain; 20cl Photolibrary/Image Source; 20tr Shutterstock/xavier gallego morel; 20c Shutterstock/Crystal Kirk; 20br Shutterstock/hypnotype; 21t Getty/Barcroft Media and the kind permission of The Stephen Wiltshire Gallery, London; 21c Getty/Barcroft Media and the kind permission of The Stephen Wiltshire Gallery, London; 21cr Photoshot/Daryl Balfour/NHPA; 21br Photoshot/Daryl Balfour/NHPA; 22bl Shutterstock/dpaint; 22tr (boy) Shutterstock/Annetta; 22tr Shutterstock/Neil Podoli; 23tr Photolibrary/fancy; 23br (maze) Photolibrary/Imagebroker; 23br Shutterstock/kak2s; 24cl & bl SPL/Jean Abitbol, ISM; 24b Shutterstock/Alekcey; 25tr SPL/Sovereign, ISM; 25c Getty/Hulton; 25cr SPL/Hank Morgan; 26c Getty/Popperfoto; 26b Shutterstock/Dainis; 27tr Getty/SSPL; 27c Corbis/Louise Gubb; 28tr SPL/James Holmes/Janssen Pharmaceutical; 28b Getty/Image Source; 29 Corbis/SPL; 31 SPL/David Parker; 32–33 Shutterstock/Zoltan Pataki; 32cl Shutterstock/Knorre; 32c Photolibrary; 33cl KF Library; 33br Shutterstock/grafvision; 33tl SPL/Juergen Berger; 33tcr SPL/Steve Gschmeissner; 33c SPL/Profs P. M. Motta, P. M. Andrews, K. R. Porter & J. Vial; 33b SPL; 33cr SPL/Marshall Sklar; 33cbr SPL/Thomas Deerinck, NCMIR; 33br Shutterstock/Sebastian Kaulitzki; 34c SPL/JJP/ Philippe Plailly/Eurelios; 34bl Shutterstock/3445128471; 35l Shutterstock/ Sebastian Kaulitzki; 35tr SPL/David Nicholls; 35b Alamy/Juniors Bildarchiv; 37tr SPL/Laguna Design; 37b (face) Shutterstock/paulaphoto; 37b (type) Shutterstock/Suzanne Long; 38–39 Shutterstock/Pedro Salaverria; 38ct SPL/Science Source; 38c SPL/A Barrington Brown; 38bl SPL/Volker Steger; 39ct Shutterstock/Studiotouch; 39cb Getty/Stone; 39br Shutterstock/Sergey Lavrentev; 40t Getty/Georges DeKeerle; 40c SPL/Larry Mulvehill; 40b SPL/BSIP/PIKO; 41l Shutterstock/kenny1; 41cl SPL/Power and Syred; 41c SPL/Eric Grave; 41cr SPL/Tek Image; 41crt Shutterstock/Leah-Anne Thompson; 41bl Shutterstock/Paul Cowan; 41br SPL/Medical RF.com; 42–43 (tree) Shutterstock/marilyn barbone; (me) Shutterstock/Simon Greig; (mom) Shutterstock/Blend Images; (dad) Shutterstock/Warren Goldswain; (grandma & granddad) Shutterstock/Supri Suharjoto; (nana) Shutterstock/Blend Images; (grandpa) Shutterstock/Alexander Raths; (granddad's parents) Shutterstock/Tudor Catalin Gheorghe; (grandma's parents) Shutterstock/frescomovie; (nana's parents) Shutterstock/Elbieta Sekowska; (grandpa's parents) Shutterstock/Tudor Catalin Gheorghe; (skeleton) Shutterstock/Jiri Vaclavek; (man) Shutterstock/gualtiero boffi; (woman) Shutterstock/Yuri Arcurs; (baby) Shutterstock/The Umf; 43c SPL/Alain Pol/ISM; 43cr SPL/Biophoto Associate; 44–45 Shutterstock/Merkushev Vasilly; 44tr Getty/New York Daily News Archive; 44tl Rex/Stuart Clarke; 44c Shutterstock/Marilyn Volan; 44c (badge) Rex/Stuart Clarke; 44bl Shutterstock/Valentin Agapov; 44bc Shutterstock/Picsfive; 45t Rex/Moscoop; 45cl Alamy/GL Archive; 45cr Getty/Hulton; 45bl Shutterstock/Arti_Zav; 45br (pen) Shutterstock/Stephanie Frey; 46tl Getty/NGS; 46cr Natural History Museum Picture Library; 46c Corbis/Sygma; 46cbl Getty/Bloomberg; 46br Natural History Museum Picture Library; 46b Alamy/Friederich Sauer; 47tr Corbis/Nikola Solic; 47ctl Corbis/Sygma; 47tc Natural History Museum Picture Library; 47c Corbis/Paul Hanna/Reuters; 47cbl Alamy/Visual&Written SL; 47b Natural History Museum Picture Library; 47br Alamy/blickwinkel; 48–49 Shutterstock; 48cl Corbis/Anthony Bannister; 49c Alamy/Photo Resource Hawaii; 49r Corbis/Martin Harvey; 49bl Corbis/Karen Kasmauski; 50 With the kind permission of Prof. Akiyoshi Kitaoka, Ritsumeikan University, Japan; 51 Getty/Reportage; 52–53 Getty/Image Bank; 52c Shutterstock/nickpit; 52b Shutterstock/David Davis; 53cr Corbis/Heritage Images; 53br Shutterstock/Amihays; 54tr Corbis/Peter Endig/epa; 54–55 Photolibrary/fStop; 54cl (eyes) Alamy/Spence Grant; 54cl Shutterstock/shcherbina galyna; 54br SPL/James King-Holmes; 55tr Alamy/Roger Bamber; 55cl Getty/NGS; 55lt Photolibrary/Stockbyte; 55c SPL/Bill Bachmann; 55cr Getty/Riser; 54–55b Shutterstock/Jason Cox; 56–57 Shutterstock/Gregor Kervina; 56t Corbis/Blue Images; 57tl Getty/Bridgeman Art Library; 57tr SPL/NYPL; 57b Shutterstock/Artpose Adam Borkowski; 58bl Photolibrary/Fancy; 58tr SPL/Arthur Toga/UCLA; 58–59 Photolibrary/Corbis; 59l Corbis/Robbie Jack; 59tr Corbis/Ocean; 59br Corbis/Anup Shah; 60tl Shutterstock/doglikehorse; 60tc Corbis/Ocean; 60tr Shutterstock/koh sze kiat; 60bl Shutterstock/doglikehorse; 60bc Shutterstock/tommiphoto; 6obr Shutterstock/doglikehorse; 61tl Corbis/Hulton; 61cr Photolibrary/Corbis; 61br PA/Alistair Grant/AP; 63cr Alamy/Simon de Trey-White; 62–63 all other images Shutterstock; 64tl Shutterstock/Karen Roach; 64–65 Shutterstock/clearviewstock; 64tr SPL/Edelmann; 64r SPL/Eye of Science; 64bl Corbis/Comet; 65tl Shutterstock/Rynio Productions; 65tc Shutterstock/Charlene Bayerie; 65tcr Shutterstock/Anastasia Bobrova; 65tr both SPL/Sovereign, ISM; 65bl Corbis/Sebastiao Moreira/Wire; 65br Corbis/Dominic Ebenbichler/Wire; 66–67 Shutterstock/tavi; 66tr Photolibrary; 66bl Alamy/moodboard; 67tr Shutterstock/fdenb; 67b Photolibrary/Phototake Science; 68–69 Corbis/Atsuko Tanaka; 68tr Alamy/Mark Pink; 68bl Shutterstock/Konstantin Sutyagin; 68br Getty/Vetta; 69tr SPL/Pasieka; 69bl Corbis/Sara De Boer/Retna; 69br Getty/Mike Ehrman; 70 Shutterstock/Blend Images; 71 Corbis/Zefa; 72cl SPL/Science Pictures Ltd.; 72r & 73l Rajeev Doshi/Medi-Mation; 73tr SPL/Mauro Fermariello; 73cr Shutterstock/zulufoto; 72–73 Shutterstock/suravid; 74tr SPL/Ralph Hutchings, Visuals Unlimited; 74b SPL/Jellyfish Pictures; 75tl, tlc, cl & bl SPL/Ralph Hutchings, Visuals Unlimited; 75cr Shutterstock/Monkey Business Images; 75br SPL/Philippe Plailly; 76 Shutterstock/Rui Vale de Sousa, Shutterstock/Samot, Shutterstock/Mazzzur; 77bl Shutterstock/Aleksandr S; 77bc Alamy/Janine Weidel; 77c Shutterstock/Petrov Anton; 77tr Getty/Gamma-Keystone; 77bc Shutterstock/Warren Goldstein; 78–79 Shutterstock/Gordon Milic, Shutterstock/angelshot, Shutterstock/J Henning Buchholz; 80–81 Shutterstock/Leigh Prather; 80tr Getty/Visuals Unlimited; 80cl SPL/Chris Bjornberg; 80cr SPL/Dr. Linda Stannard; 80bl & bc Shutterstock/Sebastian Kaulitzki; 81t SPL/Steve Gschmeisser; 81b SPL/Eye of Science; 82c SPL/Steve Gschmeisser; 82bl SPL/NIBSC; 82br SPL/3D4medical.com; 83tl Shutterstock/Nattika; 83tc Corbis/Crack Palinggi; 83tr Shutterstock/Tish1; 83br SPL/Pasquale Sorrentino; 84tl Corbis/Skip Nall; 84t Shutterstock/ouh_desire; 84tc Corbis/Wire; 84cl Shutterstock/illusionstudio; 84cb Shutterstock/Noam Armonn; 85 With the kind permission of Curtis Morton-Lowerlighter/Flickr; 85bl SPL/Eye of Science; 86–87 Shutterstock/Natallia Natykach; 86cl Alamy/les polders; 86bl Corbis/Jean Pierre Fizet; 86tr Photolibrary/Blend Images; 86c SPL/Pasieka; 86cr Shutterstock/Darren Hubley; 86cbr Getty/AFP; 86br Getty/Brand X Pictures; 86b Shutterstock/Axel Wolf; 87tl Shutterstock/Bruce L. Crandall; 87tc With the kind permission of John McCabe; 87cl Shutterstock/almond; 87c Corbis/Denis Scott; 87cr Shutterstock/Joao Virissimo; 87br Shutterstock/Yuriy_fx; 87bl Getty/AFP; 88–89 Shutterstock; 88bl Corbis/Jason Reed; 89tl Corbis/Thomas Roepke; 89tr Naturepl/Fabio Liverani; 89br Corbis/Eddie Cheng; 90 Shutterstock/Tom Wang, morphed using software at www.faceofthefuture.org.uk; 91 Getty/Bjorn Meyer; 92–93 Corbis/ Visuals Unlimited; 94–95 SPL/Steve Gschmeissner; 96 Getty/Peter Dazeley

Find out more

Recommended books

Decoding Genes with Max Axiom by Amber Keyser (Capstone Press, 2010)

Evolution Revolution by Robert Winston (Dorling Kindersley, 2009)

Kingfisher Knowledge: Genes & DNA by Richard Walker (Kingfisher Publications, 2007)

Know Your Brain by Nicola Morgan (Walker Books, 2007)

Navigators: Human Body by Miranda Smith (Kingfisher Publications, 2008)

Train Your Brain to Be a Genius by John Woodward (Dorling Kindersley, 2009)

What Goes on in My Head? by Robert Winston (Dorling Kindersley, 2010)

What Makes Me Me? by Robert Winston (Dorling Kindersley, 2010)

Recommended websites

Who Am I? at London's Science Museum:
www.sciencemuseum.org.uk/visitmuseum/galleries/who_am_i.aspx

BBC Science—Human Body and Mind: www.bbc.co.uk/science/humanbody

Becoming Human site that explores human evolution: www.becominghuman.org

How DNA Works: http://science.howstuffworks.com/environmental/life/cellular-microscopic/dna1.htm

The Human Genome Project Video—3-D Animation Introduction:
www.youtube.com/watch?v=XuUpnAz5y1g

Neuroscience for Kids: http://faculty.washington.edu/chudler/neurok.html